Problem? Solved!

Libertarian solutions for the real world

By Kent S McManigal

TIME'S UP

No more rattling- Time's Up!

By the same author...

Liberty-oriented books:
  Kent's Liberty Primer
  Tao Liberty Ching
  Indy-Pindy, The Liberty Mouse

Other:
  Sandy's Legacy, Bobwhite Quail
    in Art and Tale

Contents

Aardvarks?
Abortion
Air Travel
Animal Rights
Banking
"Big Projects"
"Blight"
Capital Punishment
Certifications and Licenses
Child Abuse
Children's Rights
Climate Change
Consumer Safety
Copyrights and Patents
Corporations
Crime
Disabled/Handicapped
Discrimination
Drunk Driving
Drug Testing and Safety
Drugs
Economy
Education
Endangered Species
Energy Costs
Environment

Evil
Families/Children
Fire Fighting
Food Inspection and Safety
Fraud
"Free Riders"
Frivolous lawsuits
Gangs
Gay Marriage
Government Corruption
Health Care
Hunger
Immigration
Inflation
Infrastructure
Jurors
Justice System
Liability
Middle East
Military
Money
Morality
National Defense
National Parks/Forests/Monuments
Pirates
Poaching
Police
Pollution
Pornography/Child Pornography
Poverty
Prisons/Prison overcrowding
Property Rights

Race Relations
Religion
Retirement
"Rich Warlord"
Roads
Sex
Space Flight
Suicide
Terrorism
Tobacco/Smoking
Trade Deficits
Transportation
Trespassing
Unemployment/Under-employment
"Vice"
Violence
Voting
War
Welfare

Abolition
Arbitration
Reputation
Restitution
Rights
Shunning
Zero Aggression Principle

Introduction- Welcome to the *solution*.

During the course of my liberty activism I have heard many people claim that *"libertarians are always whining about government being the <u>problem</u>, but they never offer <u>solutions</u>."*

I beg to differ. Solutions are offered all the time, but they are ignored because they seem "different". So be it.

However, from now on when that claim is made, stick this book in the hands of the person making the baseless assertion. That concrete action will be harder to miss.

I am not suggesting that these solutions are the *only* solutions to be found without resorting to coercion. That would be ridiculous. For most problems there are a spectrum of liberty-respecting options that could be tried or discovered. It would be impossible to anticipate them all.

If you don't like the solutions I suggest, find or create new ones. *Every* problem has solutions that complement individual liberty. You only need to look and think.

I advocate for a day when societies, and *individuals*, everywhere are free to try different liberty-respecting solutions without The State standing in the way.

I have arranged this book alphabetically, by "problem" or topic, so that it can be used as a reference book as questions arise.

As you read about one topic you may have a question about a related subject. If so, check and you may discover I have addressed that topic as well. Maybe, if I have done what I set out to do, you will find the answers you seek. I hope so.

Enjoy.

August 2010

To purchase more copies of this book go to
tinyurl.com/**ProblemSolvedLiberty**

The Problems and Issues

This first section focuses on the "problem" part of the book.

These are just some of the common problems and issues that are dredged up in conversation and used as justification for externally-imposed, coercive, government.

Many people seem to honestly feel that there can't be a solution without resorting to force.

They are wrong, as I intend to show here.

All problems have solutions that do not rely on coercion, theft, or fraud. I'll suggest some. Perhaps you will think of more.

Aardvarks?

I know you are thinking this makes no sense whatsoever... and you are right. However it does make a *point*; one important enough it deserves to be the first point made in this alphabetically-arranged book.

"Aardvarks" in this instance stand for all those things in life that are neither right nor wrong, but just "are"- like aardvarks. A comparatively small portion of your life is spent on ethical issues where a decision about "doing the right thing" must be weighed. Most of your time is devoted to things that simply *are*.

It is neither right nor wrong to cross the room, read a book, smoke some cannabis, or scratch an itch. At least as long as you are not doing one of those things as a way of avoiding something that you *should* be doing. Avoiding a responsibility or an obligation you previously agreed to (as long as it would hurt no innocent person) is wrong no matter what your excuse might be.

Don't let people confuse you by trying to pretend that their opinions or preferences are matters of "right and wrong" when they are not.

It is *wrong* to harm someone who is *innocent* (does not deserve to be harmed right now).

It is *right* to avoid doing things that are wrong, and in many cases it is right to step in to prevent an innocent from being harmed by a person or event that is threatening them.

Most other things you will encounter during your life have nothing to do with right or wrong.

Recognizing this fact will free up a lot of the time you previously spent worrying about, and concerning yourself over, what other people are doing or what *they* think about what *you* are doing. It is a trap to think every second of your life involves an ethical decision, or to waste time feeling the need to judge the lives of other people who are simply minding their own business.

Abortion

Abortion is one issue that is only good for one thing: dividing people and setting them at one another's throats. I have read libertarian positions on both sides that were absolutely *adamant* that their position was right, and that the people who held the other position were monsters.

The libertarian debate centers on just a few main points: is the embryo a *human being* with all its rights intact? ... or is it a part of the *mother's* body? ... or is it a human being, but a *trespasser* if not wanted where it exists?

I am convinced that if abortion is wrong, it would *still* be wrong even in cases of rape or incest. The embryo had no choice in the matter, and the circumstance of how you began life doesn't indicate your value as a person or your potential.

No one, *including me*, knows for certain if abortion is right or wrong, they just believe they do. That is because there is not enough scientific data to make a truly rational decision. Emotions on both sides cloud the mind and make coherent thought difficult.

A fertilized egg is life, but is not a *separate* life. There are religious *ideas* of when the embryo becomes a separate life-form from the mother, but not really any convincing scientific *proofs*. I do know that once a baby is born it is a separate life-form, a **human being**, with *all* its human rights intact (even though it is not capable of exercising them immediately).

Almost no one claims that a simple fertilized egg is a *human being* (as opposed to "human", like an organ or a hand could be), and almost no one claims that a full-term baby *isn't* one. The true dividing line is somewhere in between those extremes. No one knows for sure where it is, although many people "believe" they know where.

In case of doubt I would tend to side with the pregnant woman, whom I can readily recognize as a complete, *sentient* human being who undoubtedly has all her rights functioning. If she owns her uterus (as she does all her *other* body parts), then the baby does not own it. If the baby owns it, then the woman does not. This last position seems unworkable to me.

I realize that when the day arrives that embryos can be transplanted or put into an artificial womb at any stage of development it will make abortion, as a divisive issue, fade away. So why do "pro-life" activists not spend their time, money, and talents on designing this technology?

I think it is because they prefer to tell others how to live their lives instead. It is harder to use unwanted pregnancies to condemn a person's sex-life if the pregnancy is not a burden. In a great many cases, and from personal experience, I do think a desire to demonize sexual activity lies behind much "pro-life" activism.

This brings us to the religious objections. Almost all objections to abortion are at the core religious objections, which is fine until you try to impose your religion's values on someone else who does not share your religious views.

Murder is wrong, but does abortion qualify as murder? It seems to come down to whether or not you believe humans have "souls". And if they *do* have souls, are those souls installed at conception or sometime later? Until science has an answer, this question is up to the individual involved.

Right or wrong, "public funds" should *never* be used to finance abortions or any other medical procedures, because there is no such thing as "public funds"; it is *all* stolen ("tax") money.

I think the best intellectual exercise for thinking about this is what libertarian author and philosopher L. Neil Smith asks: Say you are right and abortion *is* murder. How do you propose to discover, regulate, and punish it? Do you make all pregnant women register to make certain that their pregnancies are not terminated?

What if you can't yet tell by looking that they are pregnant? Should all women and girls of reproductive age submit to a monthly pregnancy test to keep tabs on them? Where do you come up with the new bureaucracy, "The Department of Reproduction", to regulate pregnancy? Who pays for it?

Some people think this is taking the issue to an absurd extreme, but how many other issues have been taken to the absurd extreme once they have been judged proper issues for "legalities" and prohibition?

I have another thought that may concern men even more directly. As long as abortion is legal, men should be able to legally terminate any financial or parental responsibility for a child that they do not wish to father, right up to the time during the pregnancy where abortion would still be a legal option, and even *beyond* birth if he is intentionally kept unaware of the pregnancy. After all, that is what abortion does for women. If it is right for one person, it is right for *everyone*.

I would never send government or its agents after a person who seeks an abortion. Mostly, it comes down to the individualist attitude of *"keep your filthy government off of my life!"*

So, what is my *personal* opinion?

I don't like abortion, but would not forbid it to people who feel differently about it than I do. I do not think abortion is a good first choice for birth control. There are so many other options that are easier and cheaper.

As a male, I have obviously never had an abortion, nor have I ever encouraged anyone else to have one for any reason whatsoever. In this way I have done my part to not add to the number of abortions. Keep your own house in order and mind your own business. It's the way of Liberty.

Air Travel

Air travel, and transportation in general, are being taken over by the government to a greater degree with each passing year. Yet, bad guys will *always* manage to find a way around any "security measures" given sufficient motivation.

Airlines should be permitted to set their own policies with regard to weapons on board.

Most would undoubtedly continue to follow the poor example set by government, even though it has obviously failed tragically. *"The way we've always done it"* is a hard form of inertia from which to break free. At least it is for established and fossilized companies which have little incentive to change.

Other, possibly younger, more *innovative* companies could experiment with armed crews and passengers. Frangible ammunition, which turns to dust upon hitting a hard surface, could be sold at airports. But, that isn't really necessary. The fears based on the myth of "explosive decompression" due to a bullet hole could be defeated with proper education.

Bounties could be standard company policy in the event of a hijacking or other form of aggression on board planes.

A government "no-fly list" full of inaccuracies and politically motivated "errors" is not necessary or even helpful. Airlines could implement their own screening procedures and deny service to people they think might be dangerous, or for any other reason. Government-issued ID could be replaced by company-issued "preferred traveler" identification.

Without a "one size fits all" government agency telling airlines how they must conduct business, innovation would be free to find the best way.

It isn't all about hijackings or violence, though.

Let airlines test better options to the current air traffic controllers. Perhaps, rather than a centralized "system", let each plane have its own collision avoidance system. If the system on one plane fails, there are still multiple systems in service on other planes all around the crippled plane, watching and keeping everyone safe. It's the ultimate redundancy for safety.

Let airlines choose whether to allow smoking or not, and let the market reward the preferred policy.

Let them choose how to set their prices, and what services to offer. Let them offer the level of luxury or the no-frills economy that the customers wish to pay for.

Let them choose how much luggage, and what type, passengers may carry.

Let them innovate and offer suborbital flights, or even space flight, without begging a government agency for permission.

Stop allowing government to control (and limit) the certification of pilots. Leave that to the market and the airlines instead.

Speaking of air travel- stop allowing government to block flying cars with ridiculous requirements and red tape. The year 2000 is in our rear-view mirror, and our cars are mandated to be obsolete relics.

Animal Rights

Rights are not transferable across species lines. A rabbit has no right to not be eaten by a wolf, nor does a rabbit have a right to not be eaten, or simply *killed*, by a human.

An animal also has no right to not be abused by a predator- human or otherwise. A cat playing with a mouse is a lesson in cruelty, but the cat has no obligation to the mouse. This doesn't mean that a person who puts animals through unnecessary suffering is a wonderful person, though.

Of course, the corollary is that a human has no right to not be preyed upon by any other animal, either. Every creature, human or not, does possess the right of self-defense. Exercise it.

While a person who abuses animals is probably not a nice person, and would be a reasonable target for shunning, as long as no other human (nor the property of another) is being harmed, the abuser is within his rights.

This is another case where just because you have a *right* to do something, it may not be the *best* thing to do. You be the judge and live with the consequences of your actions.

Banking

Get government completely **out** of the financial system.

Without government encouraging "fractional reserve banking", a dishonest practice where banks lend out many times more money than they possess in reserve, banks would be much less likely to fail.

Stop forcing banks to spy on their customers for the government. Financial privacy is crucial for liberty. "Money laundering" and refusing to incriminate yourself for "taxation" purposes must not be "crimes" because they are not *wrong*.

Without an IRS for banks to report their customers to, financial liberty and security would be greatly enhanced. Wealth would be protected. The economy would flourish.

Banks should not be required to open a customer's account information or "safe deposit" boxes for agents of the government. Not under any circumstances.

Privacy and security, from *everyone*, is a bank's primary obligation to its customers. Nothing should compromise that.

"Big Projects"

Many people think that "big projects", such as roads, dams, and space programs can not exist voluntarily.

If that were really the case, then the only ethical solution is to do without them. Nothing is worth financing through theft by stealing from the productive people, and killing them if they resist.

Fortunately, coercion isn't necessary for big projects.

There are a great many people who would love to travel into space. They are willing to put large amounts of money into the hands of companies who could help them achieve the dream. Yet, government bureaucracy, specifically the FAA and NASA, stands firmly in the way of private space exploration.

The same goes for bridges, dams, and roads. If they are really needed, there will be people willing to invest money, materials, and time to see them realized. No coercion is required.

A common objection to this is that "big projects" cost more than the market will bear. When government does it, that is true. Leave out all the bureaucracy, redundant employees, and costs of enforcement and the price for anything comes way down.

Government prevents new ideas from being tried and new solutions from being found by protecting the *status quo* with "laws". That is not an optimal situation for anyone but government.

"Blight"

One man's trash is another man's treasure.

Many people like to cover their property with the things they have collected over the course of their lifetime, or with the refuse of their household, while others want to be surrounded with neatly mowed lawns and uniform fences and mailboxes. This causes conflict.

To avoid this problem, people could choose to only live in an area which has certain rules, adopted by **unanimous** *consent*, concerning clutter. Or they could choose to build high fences, since "good fences make good neighbors".

If a person's "treasures" are straying from his property, then he is harming the property of another. The same is true if unwelcome creatures are attracted to his clutter and end up becoming a problem for neighbors.

In this case, the neighbors should ask the property owner if he would like help cleaning up. If he is happy with his property just as it is, the neighbors could attempt to "buy him out" or even offer him money to clean up.

If this all fails, the neighbors could seek arbitration.

In other cases, the "blight" might concern old buildings that have fallen into disrepair, or which have been decorated in ways that offend the neighbors. Many of the same methods could be employed to deal with this as well.

However, a lot of "blight" is simply a problem of people not minding their own business and thinking they have a right to control the behavior or property of others. Remember to ask yourself "Who is being harmed?" Remember, too, that "harm" is physical or financial damage, not "offense".

Capital Punishment

Capital punishment is nothing but revenge institutionalized. It is dead wrong; no pun intended.

If you are being attacked, you have the absolute right to fight back in any way you need to in order to end the attack. I would even support your decision to use deadly force to stop vandalism or theft in almost all cases, since property crimes are stealing your life and security.

Death at the hands of the victim, or an individual who intervenes at the scene of the attack, is a fair outcome for someone who has decided to initiate force. However, once the aggressor leaves the scene, there will always be some doubt, *some*where, as to guilt. Especially if the only witness is dead, as is the case in many "capital crimes".

No government *anywhere* is so pure or honest that it should be trusted with the authority to decide to kill someone as punishment. Once a person is caught and charged with a crime, all the government cares about is conviction.

The fact that many defendants are found "not guilty", *despite* the best efforts of the jury-tampering judges, shows that the system can still work on occasion. However, no jury is above being influenced by a judge or prosecutor who is looking to advance his career by being seen as "tough on crime".

Governments lie. They manufacture evidence, intimidate witnesses, play on some people's "authority worship", and set-up innocent people who dare to stand against their edicts. Show me a perfect, just government that I would trust with power over life and death, and I will show you a government that has no desire for revenge.

Imprisonment helps no one, and doesn't produce justice, however, if no restitution is possible due to death or disfigurement, and there is no doubt about guilt because of a confession or other absolute proof, prison might still play some role in a free society. If a defendant is known to be guilty of a "capital" crime, send him to prison for life and, since there is no "taxation", let those who believe in his innocence, his family, or even his victims, pay for his upkeep.

Or if no imprisonment compromise can be reached, let him roam free and try to survive surrounded by people who know who he is and what he did, and he may not survive long-especially if he strikes again. In this age of the internet, there is nowhere to hide, and in a free society helpless victims will be hard to come by.

Certifications and Licenses

It is not necessary to have a governmental bureaucracy certifying a business or a person's proficiency at a skill. Industry experts and qualified individuals could do a better job.

Who knows whether a hairdresser knows their business? Other hairdressers and satisfied (or not) customers or some bureaucrat?

There could be competing certifying organizations to prevent cronyism and favoritism from destroying fairness. The certifiers who do the best job, as judged by the skills of those they certify, would gain a reputation for trustworthiness. Others, if they did not do as well, would fall out of favor and be avoided by customers and people looking for certification alike.

It would be the same for electricians, doctors, plumbers, or any job that requires a level of proficiency and trust.

Government certification is not a good standard, and one size *never* fits all.

Child Abuse

That which qualifies as child abuse to some would be called "discipline" by others. (**"Sex"** is covered elsewhere) Even some parentally-instilled beliefs could be seen as mental abuse, especially when the child is being indoctrinated with attitudes and beliefs that give him a deeply flawed view of reality.

There should be no government agency or bureaucracy empowered with taking children from parents, not even in cases of real harm. This system is too easy to abuse for coercive purposes. Instead, that power lies with the rest of the family and with individuals who are aware of the true situation.

In a free society, if you witness a person of any age or ability being attacked you would be free to intervene. You can deal with the consequences later. In cases where your justifications for your actions are disputed, arbitration could settle the matter. If bruises or other injuries seem to indicate abuse is occurring, those who are suspicious could either hire an arbitrator on the child's behalf, or find one willing to donate his time.

If a child is being abused, let the child decide whether to stay in the situation or find a better one. Which leads into the next topic...

Children's Rights

Children have the same rights as anyone else. However, they are unable to exercise their rights fully right away. They have the rights, but their freedom is limited by their ability. They have increasing freedom and liberty as they gain abilities to exercise those rights without encroaching on the rights of others.

This is different than the practice of authoritarians violating the rights of responsible people by claiming they "might hurt themselves or someone else" because children, up to a certain level of development (which varies from person to person), actually *do* need help or they would not survive.

Even the youngest child has the right to not be harmed. The child doesn't necessarily have the right to force a parent to take care of her, but a parent has the obligation to either take care of the children brought into the world by his actions, or find someone else who will.

What about discipline?

In some cases "spanking" might be justified as a response to the child initiating force, but in many cases it would obviously be wrong. If you can think of nothing other than violence to help your child grow up to be a responsible, accountable person who respects the rights of those around him, then your parenting tool kit is in need of more tools. It is a sign that you may have already failed in your task.

Some parents remain absolutely convinced that to "spare the rod" will "spoil the child". Others might see this as an attack on an innocent person by you.

Someone might even step in to rescue your child from your initiation of force, and the two of you might end up in a physical confrontation or arbitration to settle the matter. This is one of the times you do what you think is right, and accept the consequences if it turns out you are wrong.

Climate Change

One common justification for the "climate change" hysteria is that even if the climate change believers turn out to be *wrong*; either that there *is* climate change, or that it is caused by *human activities*, there is little harm in taking the prescribed corrective measures. That is absolute nonsense!

Little harm? The "solution" for "*anthropogenic global climate change*", demanded by the collectivists who falsely call themselves "environmentalists", destroys the ability of regular people to earn a living. It puts the world's very worst polluters, *governments*, in charge of telling everyone else how to live, and punishing those among us who disobey.

It does *worse* than sending humanity back to the stone age, since at least back then *they* had fire with which to cook food, light the dark, and heat themselves.

It sets up a new caste system, where the politically powerful, rich, and/or connected get to maintain a modern lifestyle, while "the little people" are expected to sacrifice most of the advances of the past several hundred years for "the common good", while still being expected to not be as "messy" as our forebears.

It also terrifies some people much like the "nuclear annihilation" threat of an earlier generation did. That is an awful *lot* of harm.

Modern society is remarkably clean. Only government deals and favoritism (known as "corporatism") keep the big polluters (corporations and government) from taking full *individual* responsibility for their actions, and making full restitution for their mistakes and misdeeds.

The modern individual leaves less mess behind than the primitive individual did. It is just that there are an awful lot of us humans now, and we are being artificially *forced*, by government fear and inertia, to stay in our planetary cradle instead of being allowed to naturally spread out from Earth as would probably be occurring by now.

The best way to do what you can for the environment, including the planetary climate, hasn't changed: Don't soil your own nest, and take full, *individual*, responsibility for the mess you *do* make when it harms the property or lives of others.

In the interest of full disclosure, I would be happy to live in a cave under primitive conditions.

Or in a tipi or a dugout.

No electricity or running water (or, as I used to tell my first ex-wife *"we'd have electricity during thunderstorms, and running water when it rains...."*).

The thought doesn't bother me at all.

However, I know most people don't feel that way. Many people depend on modern advances for their very *lives*. I have no business taking their non-coercive choices from them. Neither does anyone else.

Consumer Safety

Buyer beware. Does this stop being true because there are government employees and stacks of applicable "laws" regulating products and services? Of course not.

The most reputable and famous testing lab is not affiliated with government, and it does a great job. You can always choose to buy *un*tested, and possibly cheaper, products. You often get what you pay for.

In an absence of government regulations there would probably be many more testing labs opening up. Probably specializing in certain areas of expertise. Some would be good, and some would not. I would learn which ones to trust through my own experiences and by talking to other people. Just as I often do now.

In a free society if a product or service causes harm, the individuals responsible would be individually accountable. There would be no "liability caps" or "corporation" to hide behind.

This accountability would help ensure adequate testing and the assigning (and *acceptance*) of responsibility when something goes wrong. Denial or delay would only result in more harm and higher eventual restitution.

Copyrights and Patents

Intellectual property ("IP"), the idea that a person's creative works belong to them even after copies have been distributed, is a fairly new thing.

Throughout most of human history when a person invented something, or made up a poem or song, once anyone else was introduced to that new creation they could, and would, copy the original and no one thought anything of it. Before industrialization this was how progress was spread.

I doubt anyone panicked about someone else stealing their design for the wheel or idea for "agriculture"; two examples of things that are much more important than the newest incarnation of the "legally-protected" movie franchise or song.

Then some lawyer had an idea. He would get "laws" enacted to give a person control over their own creation so that they alone would profit from it (after paying the lawyer and government a hefty fee, of course)- at least for a while.

I can understand someone wanting to profit from their creations. I know it would be a nice situation to be in, but is it *right* to use government to do so? I have witnessed many heated discussions among libertarians about "IP", and have read good points from both sides of the fence. The two positions come down to this:

"Once you buy that CD/book/program you should be able to do anything with it, including copying it and selling the copies. What right does anyone have to tell you what you can do with your own property?" And *"You can't own what is inside another person's head. Once you communicate your idea to him, in whatever way, he owns the copy inside his own head, to do with as he wishes."*

vs.

"The artist put a lot of work into creating the content of that CD/book/program, and the recording company/publisher/software company invested a lot of money to produce it. They should profit from their effort and investment, and that profit should be protected for a while."

It doesn't take government to protect "IP", of course, but many find it hard to think of free market solutions. Is "protection" justified by property rights, or would that violate the property rights of the person who bought the CD or book? Does the elimination of "IP" protection destroy the incentive to create?

I know that some of my creations have been used here and there, most with attribution; some without. It doesn't really bother me too much. Of course, there isn't any real money at stake either. Would I feel differently if I stood to gain or lose a lot of money? Probably, because I am human.

Does that settle the matter? Absolutely not. My personal feelings or wishes have no bearing on the issue.

My opinion is that "Intellectual Property" is a nice idea for the creative person, but is probably unrealistic as we head into the post-government era of easily copied "content". "IP" was probably an anomalous blip on the time-line of human history; one which has just about run its course.

I don't worry too much about protecting my own "IP", but, as a courtesy, I try very hard to not dishonestly benefit from the "IP" of others. "*Do unto others...*" and all that.

Corporations

Most businesses are pretty good. Most try hard to give a good product or service for the price charged. In a free society with a free market, their survival depends on it. Then again, in the regulated economy we have today, some do not do this. Most of the bad players just happen to be corporations.

Corporations are in actuality a fictional invention of the government, and act as a branch that can not be separated from that governmental trunk. Remember *that* before you place blame on *honest* businesses.

Corporations depend on governmental favors and exemptions that should not exist in a market. They lobby for "laws" that stifle their competition and establish tax-rate disparities. The free market has nothing *whatsoever* to do with corporations.

Some people fear that without a government putting rules in place to protect the corporation's owners and employees that they wouldn't take risks that might turn out to be very profitable or absolutely disastrous gambles.

I think there are plenty of ways to protect individual owners, employees, and investors without corporatism stacking the deck.

There is a difference between an honest mistake, negligence, and intentional dishonesty. Each should have its own level of restitution involved.

Each person would also have a different degree of liability. The inspector who noticed and ignored the metal shavings in the cereal would shoulder more blame than the president of the company who really does try to provide the best possible product at the lowest possible price in order to make the most profit. The investor who knew nothing about the operations of the factory would share no blame, but might still lose his investment if the company loses its reputation and customers.

Reputation and trust are precious and can't be simulated or forced on anyone. Individual responsibility is essential in building them.

Crime

People seem terrified of crime. Many think it would spread like wildfire if government were not there to punish it. That isn't true at all.

"Crime" is just anything the government doesn't approve of. It could be right or wrong, or even morally and ethically neutral.

Many hideously evil acts are not "crimes" if they are committed by government agents, and many truly good things *are* "crimes" just because the government says so.

The fact is that most "criminals" didn't start out harming innocent people. They started out by doing things that did not involve aggression, theft, or fraud, but were simply prohibited by government. Just as *you* do every day, possibly without even knowing. When they were caught they were placed into a society where they learned attitudes and skills from people who actually *did* commit aggression, theft, or fraud. In other words, they were sent to "Criminal University"; which is euphemistically called "prison".

The easiest way to prevent crime is to stop criminalizing things that do not harm an innocent third party. No victim; no crime.

Since the people doing these things are no longer "offenders", they don't get exposed to people who would teach them worse habits.

Then, all acts of self-defense need to be normalized once again. It is natural and right to defend yourself from attacks and theft. "Laws" that criminalize this natural and right behavior only make aggressors safer. Safer aggressors mean more of them and less safety for the good people.

Gun control is a direct cause of much of the aggression in our society. Bad people do not obey "laws" regulating guns, but some good people unwisely do. This makes it less likely that an attacker will find himself facing an armed intended victim.

The solution to crime is obvious, and within easy reach.

If an act intentionally harms an innocent person it is wrong. If it does not, then "laws" prohibiting it are wrong and must be removed.

And most accidents must stop being treated as "crime". Not every tragedy needs to be a "crime" or needs to involve "the law" since to heap punishment on top of tragedy is cruel and pointless. The next tragedy will *not* be prevented by punishing a victim of a previous one.

Disabled/Handicapped

Should "laws" require every business to be modified to suit people with disabilities? Of course not.

Business owners should be free to cater to whomever they wish. People should be free to patronize any business they want, subject only to the wishes of the business owner. The property rights of the business owner trump the wishes of the individual customer. The right of association is paramount. No one should be forced to associate with anyone they would rather not, for any reason.

Most business owners would probably do what they can afford to do to accommodate everyone they can. It makes good business sense. That might mean instructing employees to supply extra help to those who need it, or it might mean putting a ramp through the curb.

The solution is to recognize that not everyone can afford every type of accommodation. "Laws" requiring accommodation hurt everyone in the long run. There is no way to anticipate every individual's needs and wishes. Let businesses and individuals adjust and adapt to find what works for them in each situation.

With employment, it is obvious that some people, through no fault of their own, are not physically or mentally capable of doing certain jobs. I have limits just as does everyone else.

To force an employer to hire, or continue to employ, someone who can not properly (or safely) do their job is ridiculous. Everyone can do *something*, but no one can do *everything*. That is reality and people need to accept it.

Discrimination

Each and every one of us has an absolute right of association. Some may choose to exercise this in a way that offends others. As long as he is not initiating force, defrauding anyone, trespassing, or stealing from others, what the discriminator does is within his rights, even if you think it is *not nice*.

You have a basic human right to hire, rent to, or do business with anyone you want for any reason at all, or even for *no* reason. No one has the authority to order you to do otherwise.

However, as with many other things, by exercising your right in certain ways you will set yourself up for consequences you may find disagreeable.

If you choose to discriminate based upon something arbitrary, such as race, sex, orientation, religion, or ethnic background, you give others a good reason to discriminate against *you* as well. Some people may deeply resent your discrimination and choose to let others know about it, while shunning you and your business. They may picket you, and as long as they do not trespass on someone's property, it is within their rights to do so. Other people may agree with you and choose to give you extra business. In a free society you get to decide whether the benefits outweigh the drawbacks.

Drunk Driving

What could be done about drunk drivers in a free society?

There are lots of solutions.

First of all, as long as no one has been *harmed*, there has been no "wrong" committed. "*Might harm someone*" is an open invitation to tyranny.

There are a great many things that can cause as much or more impairment than alcohol or other chemicals. Emotions, exhaustion, sudden distractions, boredom, and other things all affect the ability of a driver to remain focused. To single out, for punishment, one or two causes is ridiculous.

It is each person's responsibility to not only avoid causing harm to the innocent, but also to watch out for their *own* safety. If you see a driver who seems erratic it is your responsibility to avoid him. The responsibility can fall on *no one* else. Ever.

Since any "driver certification" (which would replace "driver's licenses" in a free society) would be up to independent companies, possibly in conjunction with insurance, they could have their own requirements as to when you are not allowed to drive if you are to remain "covered" under your agreement. If a person has a history of alcohol abuse their certification might require a breathalyzer-controlled ignition.

Other people might choose similar ways to prevent themselves from driving when they would be unable to be safely alert, aware, and in control.

There would be no more of The State defining down "drunk driving" with lower and lower "blood-alcohol content" levels until it is utterly meaningless, as has become the case.

No more freedom-to-travel-violating "checkpoints" operated as fishing expeditions by LEOs looking to increase their revenue.

Cars could be equipped with automatic crash-avoidance systems. Charities could offer free rides home without any risk of running afoul of the "law". Those engaging in sensible behavior, such as "sleeping it off" in a car on the side of the road, would not be running a risk of arrest.

And, finally, if a driver *does* cause harm, for *any* reason, restitution would be owed. No jail time; no arrest; no negotiating or plea bargains with anyone other than the harmed party or their survivors. Just restitution.

Drug Testing and Safety

Drug testing *can* save people from suffering bad effects from new, untested drugs, while looking for evidence of whether the new drug has any benefit.

However, the too-often ignored flip-side is that drug testing as currently mandated by The State kills many people with unnecessary delays. It also increases suffering among, and removes potential treatment options from, people who are suffering from terminal diseases by "protecting" them from unproven drugs. This is crazy.

There is no rational reason why only government can or should oversee drug testing. Kill the monopoly.

Private labs would do a better job of testing drugs. Desperate patients should be allowed to try any medication they wish, as long as they understand the risks. Doctors should not be prevented from using everything in their arsenal that they think has a chance of working, and that the patient wants to try.

Informed consent should be the standard, not bureaucracy and regulation.

Drugs

End the War on Drugs. Completely. Re-legalize all "drugs", once again, just as they were legal *before*. Don't "regulate and tax"; just get out.

The War on Drugs has completely *failed* to reduce drug abuse. Addiction rates are still unchanged after about a century of prohibition.

Illegal drugs are just chemicals the government doesn't want you to put in your body.

Either you control your own body, or you do not. It has *never* been within the legitimate authority of anyone to decide what another person can put into his body. Trying to assert that false authority causes tragedy.

Abusing drugs is a stupid thing to do. Yet, so is abusing food, electronic entertainment, or "authority". Of these, only the abuse of "authority" harms other people more than it harms the abuser.

If you have a problem concerning abuse of a substance, and you want to solve it, seek help. It helps if you can do so without fear of the life-destroying consequences of the legal system that is inherent in prohibition.

The crime associated with drug abuse, and used as the justification for the war, is actually caused by the *prohibition*, and has skyrocketed in some places. Aggressive violence *always* goes hand-in-hand with prohibition, whether it is the "Mexican cartels" or the turf wars between gangs in America.

Prohibition raises prices, which gives an incentive to take the risks and attracts risk-seeking personality types who don't worry about consequences. Violence is used among these people in order to protect their share of the market; that violence often spills over into the rest of society, and creates justifications for violating the rights of people who are not even *using* the prohibited substances.

If a person attacks another person or steals property, address *that* issue and stop the violations of our human rights that come from a war that is wrong at its very foundation.

Some don't wish to understand, but it isn't "giving in" when you realize you have been heading in the opposite direction from where you need to go and you turn around; rather it is "coming to your senses".

The only ones opposed to this are those whose jobs, status, and livelihoods depend on rushing full-steam down this wrong track, and those they have fooled. Don't be one of these.

Economy

The economy is self-correcting unless government steps in to stop the corrections. Through government actions a "slow economy" can turn into a depression or hyperinflation. To save the economy, government must get out of the way. Government doesn't need to "help" individuals or small business, it just needs to get out of the way and *stop actively hurting* them.

One crucial step is to eliminate the Federal Reserve and stop its printing presses. Counterfeiting isn't any better when government (or a quasi-governmental gang in this case) does it.

Through the Federal Reserve's actions, the dollar has lost around 96% of its value so far. Look for the trend to continue to erode those last four cents. Each new dollar that is printed or electronically created makes the dollar in your wallet or bank account worth just a little less. The mountains of fictitious money handed out in "bailouts" will devastate your financial future as soon as it trickles down and permeates society. Thanks to the "bailouts" and the "stimulus", it is now unavoidable.

Only a gold standard, preferably with no "official currency", can save America's financial future now.

This rational solution would take power from the US government and its pet "banksters", so it will not even be considered. That is unfortunate.

The good news is that you can still protect yourself from the worst of the consequences, even without "official" sanction.

When the hyperinflation that *will* result from the US government's counterfeiting operation hits, stop accepting US dollars as payment for anything. *Immediately*; without worrying that you will offend someone or look crazy. Otherwise you will be working for free- trading value for nothing.

Only by taking this action, or by stocking up on silver, gold, and non-perishable goods now, can you protect yourself in the coming collapse. Hoarding, saving, or investing "dollars" will not help you when those dollars lose the last bit of value they still retain.

Education

Education is *much* too important to leave to government.

"Public schools" have become government indoctrination camps. Students are trained to accept the *status quo* and never question the foundations upon which it is built. Students learn to conform their bodies to arbitrary schedules, enforced and reinforced with bells, and to accept the word of the classroom Ruler as Law.

Fortunately, children are strong enough that the "success" rate isn't 100%.

In the days *before* compulsory government schooling, literacy rates in America were high.

Now, after more than a century of government schooling, graduates are barely literate and have little or no comprehension of math, science, or history. They are unable to think logically, or critically, or to evaluate ideas on their merit. They *do* have an attitude of entitlement, however. And possibly "self esteem".

They are also well-qualified to work at menial jobs where they can earn just enough to stay alive, with the help of the welfare programs they are encouraged to use.

It's a great system for getting people to think of government as inevitable and necessary, but it is terrible for teaching them to be fully-realized humans.

Compulsory schooling is a bad idea. Does being held prisoner against your will by a teacher make you hungry for knowledge? Not every person needs or wants the same sort of education, nor are they all interested in the same subjects. What if the school doesn't offer education in subjects that interest you? What if you have always just wanted to be a pastry chef; do you still need to know what year a particular Chinese dynasty ended? Why isn't that choice up to you? Why not teach people how to find the information they may be interested in once it becomes important to them to know?

People should be able to choose. Self ownership is inalienable and should never be violated. Especially not "for your own good".

"Public schools" are financed through property "taxes"; which is a fancy way of referring to a ransom on your house. Pay up or the thugs will come steal your home, and kill you if you resist. What lesson does this teach the kids who are aware of it?

If you want to teach kids that it isn't good to be a thug, it helps if you are not a *thug*.

Endangered Species

The mindset of government with regard to endangered species can be illustrated by what happened when some "ivory smugglers" were caught a few years ago.

In order to "save the elephants", trade in ivory is very tightly controlled. This causes a shortage and gives incentives to people to take the risk of being caught. And some *were* caught with a large harvest. Now a government had "confiscated" (stolen) tons of this precious material from the "poachers".

So, what did the government do to "save" elephants? They *burned* the ivory, thus ensuring the price would stay inflated enough to make "poaching" profitable, and ensuring that the dead elephants died completely in vain. There, in a nutshell, is how governments believe (or pretend) they will save endangered species.

Had all that ivory entered, and *flooded*, the market, the price would have gone down and would have made the indiscriminate killing of elephants less attractive. If the elephants were owned by individuals, who could farm them for a profit, elephants would be much safer from extinction.

Private individuals can do *much* better, as

numerous examples illustrate.

The American bison was almost extinct when a few concerned ranchers rounded up some of the last individuals and began breeding them. This did more to save the species than protecting a few in national parks did, or could *ever* have done. This avoided the problem of putting all your eggs (or bison) in one basket.

Now bison are bred for meat and hides and there are now hundreds of thousands of them. Not roaming *free*, for the most part, but still saved from extinction. Government regulations from one agency or another still stand in the way of free-ranging bison over most of the country.

People will save and protect that which has value to them. For some it is monetary value; for others it is aesthetic or spiritual value.

If you simply pass "laws" making it a "crime" to kill something, or to alter its habitat, you encourage the "*shoot, shovel, and shut up*" tactic that many property owners must adopt in order to protect their property rights from meddlesome bureaucrats. This doesn't help the species at all, but endangers them even more.

Energy costs

Energy surrounds us. Most of it goes to waste. It doesn't need to be expensive. So, why is it? Regulation, red tape, and protectionism.

Get rid of the Department of Energy as a first step. Eliminate all "taxes" on fuels and energy. Stop subsidizing any form of energy production. Do not maintain or establish government-mandated monopolies.   Separate science and State. Let the market find novel solutions.

It might be in new sources of energy, new ways to harness or use known energy, or in more efficient products where so little energy is consumed that it can be collected from any source.

As long as an inventor is not harming anyone, there should be no interference with his experimentation.

There is no such thing as "perpetual motion", no matter what you may have read in those forwarded emails decrying the conspiracy to "keep down" the motors that run forever without fuel. However, with energy everywhere it is only a matter of time, with a free society, until something almost as grand is uncovered. Government only has to stay out of the way and let science, and the market, work.

Environment

It has always struck me as ironic to the point of insanity that some "environmentalists" expect the world's *worst polluter*, the government, to tell the rest of us how we should take care of the environment. Then that polluter gets to collect "fines" (more stolen money) for its own treasury when it decides someone has polluted.

If a person destroys their own property, which is always part of the right of ownership, then that person has lost some of the value of their property in case of wanting to sell it at some time in the future. If that doesn't matter to them, then it shouldn't matter to you.

People usually take care of that which they own. And even in cases where they *don't*, unless their filth encroaches on another person's property it is no one's business. Obviously, it is quite difficult to be filthy and keep it all contained on your own land, so there is an incentive to watch your pollution and keep it in check.

If a factory or a neighbor produces pollutants, and those leave his property, either above ground, in the air, or by contaminating ground water, the polluter owes restitution to the individuals he has harmed. Individually. For the full amount of the damages. Investigators, hired by the harmed individual, could trace the source of pollutants. Arbitration could determine the damages if the polluter refused to take responsibility. If, even after arbitration, he refused to live up to his obligations, then shunning and ostracism would be in order. To the point of starving him to death if necessary.

If you fear that a neighbor might *start* polluting and damage you, you are free to offer to buy his property from him. You might even get together with other people who have an interest in keeping him away to pool your funds to buy him out.

This same approach can also work in cases of "blight" or ruining your scenic view.

Evil

When I use the word "evil" I am referring to any act which harms an innocent person. And, by "innocent" I mean someone who does not deserve to be harmed at this moment. No one is "innocent" all the time, nor is *anyone* never "innocent". All you can do is judge their innocence or guilt at this moment, based upon their actions.

How does liberty solve the problem of evil? By taking away the most dangerous tool evil uses to inflict its harm: the cloak of legitimacy.

A person who commits evil acts is normally only a danger to people who are proximate to him. He is also likely to be eliminated from a free society fairly soon if he commits evil acts very often. At some point, odds are that he will attempt to harm someone who is prepared to defend himself.

However, let that person gain "authority" by becoming a part of government, and the evil he commits can be spread beyond his personal sphere. The greater the "authority"; the greater the danger from his evil acts. Soon this person will be insulated from the consequences of his actions by layer upon layer of "laws", and protected from individual acts of self defense by armed guards paid with the money taken, by force or threat of force, from the very people he is harming.

It is insanity to set up a system that is so attractive to those who have a desire to control and coerce other people. It will, by its very nature, attract those least able to resist the lure of committing evil acts with little risk of consequence.

Government either *attracts* damaged people who thrive on forcing their will on others, or it causes people to become that way. Either way, wherever it exists it becomes a dangerous tool in the hands of damaged individuals bent on domination.

De-legitimizing the false "authority" inherent in government brings evil back down to a place where it can be controlled on an individual basis. One act of self defense at a time. It makes evil risky again.

Families/Children

Family members do not own one another; not even the children are the property of the parents. Parents do have a right to raise their children as they see fit, no matter what others might think, as long as they do not initiate force against the children. Does this automatically mean "no spanking"? Not necessarily. Remember that word "initiate". Sometimes force is the appropriate response to force.

A free society would probably err on the side of the rights of the parents to live as they see fit. There might sometimes be tragedies as a result of this freedom, but that will always happen no matter what and fails as justification for The State's presumed ownership of all "minor children".

Children begin life unable to take care of themselves. Completely helpless. Parents have the responsibility to provide for the care of their children. Sometimes this means giving the children to another family which is better suited to care for them. The government should have no say in adoptions. When children are responsible enough to declare they no longer wish to be their parents' responsibility, and have the means to act on this decision, they should be allowed to go. Once again, the government should have no say.

Fire Fighting

There is no rational reason why government should have a monopoly on fire fighters. In fact, they don't, even *now*, although you would never know that from many people's objections to having a free society without coercive funding for fire departments. Like the "police", this is an area where some people can't seem to think freely.

In a free society fire fighting could be a subscription service. You could contract with one of the competing local fire departments to protect you and your property from fire damage. They might provide fire detectors and automated fire suppression systems to help prevent or limit damage, since in many cases they could be responsible for paying for any damage they allowed to occur to their clients' property. They might also refuse to contract with a person who refuses to avoid potentially dangerous practices or who has too many fires. Careful clients could get discounts.

There is a more comprehensive explanation of how free market fire fighting could work under "**Free Riders**" where it is my first example.

Food Inspection and Safety

Have you ever realized that meat products that meet USDA standards are barely edible? Every meat producer that has *good* products exceeds, by leaps and bounds, the government's standards.

I suspect the same is true of all businesses that produce food. The government standard is the bare minimum and is not nearly good enough.

The foods "passed" for public school lunches would fail to pass the test for any common fast food outlet's meals. That is why private businesses, even with compulsory government inspection, have their own inspectors and standards. They know what their customers want and it is in their best interest to provide it to the best of their ability.

If private industry can do so much better even now, why continue with the archaic system of letting government employees inspect?

As in any other example, let private businesses arise to provide competing health and safety inspections for food providers, hold businesses (and owners) responsible for any harm they might cause, and let customers choose who they trust and rely upon.

Fraud

When I talk about "fraud" I am referring to the use of lies or other forms of deception in order to facilitate an interaction when the truth would have caused one party to refuse to participate. It may not "initiate force", but it is still *wrong*. It is something I know I should not do to other people, and if I do, I deserve to have the same done to me.

Now, I also think it is fine and noble to lie to someone who has initiated lies, or is credibly threatening coercion. Would I lie to protect "Jews in the attic"? Absolutely. And if that didn't work, I'd *kill* to protect them. Is it wrong to lie to a liar or an attacker? I don't think so. Is it wrong to cause harm to an innocent person? Obviously it is. In many cases fraud is an economic lie and it causes harm to innocent people.

If someone paints a passable copy of the Mona Lisa, signs it with da Vinci's name, and then offers it for sale- caveat emptor. Da Vinci is dead and probably isn't too worried about his own "Intellectual Property".

If you only want the Mona Lisa because you like the way it looks, then a copy is fine. That is why prints sell. If you buy the *original* Mona Lisa you are attempting to buy more than just its physical appearance; you are wanting to buy its history and its ..... aura. That may be a difficult to understand desire to some other people, but it's your choice.

For the seller to set the price based upon the pretense that a copy is the original is to sell something that isn't really a part of the package. You are not getting everything you are paying for. In the case of the copy there is no "history" going along with the painting. Leonardo's hands did not touch the actual, physical item you hold, and if that is part of why you want it, you have been cheated. I state again: *caveat emptor*, but to fall for a fraud isn't wrong any more than being the victim of a mugging would be. I know that to cheat people is wrong, even if they are gullible.

Now, what kind of action would be justified? Restitution. And if the defrauder refuses, then shunning and public airing of the fraud would be appropriate. I wouldn't be comfortable with saying that a person who defrauds you is fair game for you to shoot in self-defense. Although, depending on the circumstances, I might not judge against someone who *does* shoot a perpetrator of fraud if I were the arbitrator.

"Free Riders"

A "free rider" is someone who gets a benefit from a service or infrastructure that they didn't contribute toward. Many people find free riders to be their main objection to a society based on voluntary contribution rather than coerced taxation.

I have had people pose the objection that in a free society, where one would contract voluntarily with a private fire department, if your neighbor's house catches fire and your fire department fights it in order to save *your* house from damage, the neighbor has benefited from your contract without paying anything. That is true, as far as it goes.

I suppose you could have a stipulation that your fire department is to not fight fires consuming your neighbors' houses, if they have not *also* contracted for service, so as not to contribute to their "free-riderhood". The fire department could just sit at your house, hosing it down so the fire doesn't spread to your property. As long as the contract was agreeable to you and your fire department, I suppose you could have just about any conditions put in you like.

Alternately, if your house catches fire and your fire department puts it out, your neighbor has still benefited, since his house is less likely to be damaged now. Or would you prefer that in this case, your fire department set fire to the neighbor's house after extinguishing yours in order to allow nature to take its course? No, I don't really think anyone would want that.

Perhaps a fire department could extinguish a non-subscriber's flames and then send a bill for services rendered. If payment is made, then there was no free rider. If payment is *refused*, then everyone knows whom to not help in the future.

Basically, I think the problem is greatly exaggerated. If people get together to build a bridge, and don't charge a toll for crossing it, does that mean an out-of-town visitor is a "free rider" if he crosses the bridge? He may be crossing the bridge to trade with a business owner who helped pay for the bridge; someone he wouldn't have been able to trade with had the bridge not been built. So is the business owner being cheated since he paid to help build the bridge and the visitor did not?

What if this person who crosses the bridge decides to trade with a business owner who *also* didn't contribute to the construction of the bridge? Does this "free riding" business owner *never* trade with the other businesses in town? How did he get the money that he spends in these other stores? Is there no value in keeping his store open for the other people in town? Do his neighbors not benefit from him and his business being there?

If people see a benefit for something, they will probably be willing to foot the bill. In a free society, bridges and roads and fire departments would undoubtedly be cheaper and better, since no bureaucracy is eating up the funds and producing nothing but more bureaucracy.

There is no reason to whip out coercion to deal with this. A true parasite will suffer the consequences of his decisions regardless of whether there is a "government" of any sort to punish him or not.

Besides, *everyone* will be the "free rider" at times. There is no avoiding it. I think this is only a problem if you look at the situation selfishly or from a "but that's not *fair*" perspective. Just accept that the times someone else is getting a "free ride" on your dime are paybacks for the times you get the same benefit.

It all comes out even in the end, so don't keep a ledger trying to nit-pick every offense. Even if someone seems to come out ahead, are you *really* willing to give up a little of your liberty to make sure everyone pays in every instance? *I'm* not.

Frivolous lawsuits

A great many offenses could be dealt with by suing the guilty party. It isn't necessary to involve government. Yes, as it *now* stands this requires using the government-owned courts, but that isn't the way it *must* be. For justice to occur, courts *must* be separated from government, especially in cases where government is one of the involved parties.

One thing that a true justice system, based on restitution to the injured party, *must* include is a requirement that the loser pay all the court costs, as well as any revenue lost by the winner as a result of the lawsuit.

No "public funds" would be used to run the court- true costs would be reflected in the price the losing party pays.

Then, let anyone sue for anything they want, with the understanding that if the court/jury finds their suit *frivolous*, or if they are found to be in the wrong, they will be the one paying all the expenses and restitution to the target of their suit.

After a couple of nonsensical lawsuits, no one would be willing to deal with the suit-happy individual any longer; not wanting to risk being sued for looking at the person wrong, or serving hot coffee that is actually *hot*. No one would want to rent to them, or from them.

Plus, unless they were already wealthy, they couldn't afford to keep losing and paying their victims. After a while, even the privately owned courts might refuse to accept their cases.

The litigious individual would likely find themselves *shunned*, and would lose any suit based on being "discriminated against" as this is a basic right *all* people have: the **right of association**. They would become outcasts out of fear that they are simply looking for a reason to sue someone so that they can "win the lottery". That would not be a good strategy for a person to adopt in a free society.

Gangs

Gangs are primarily financed through profits from "drug" prohibition and other black market niches, such as providing stolen guns to those "legally prohibited" from possessing them.

They are also enabled by our society's dangerous habit of segregating the young from general society and grouping them with others of their own age group, creating an "*us* vs. *them*" culture, in schools.

End the "War on (some) Drugs" and end compulsory government schooling and you have pulled the foundation out from under the gangs.

Then eliminate any and all prohibitions on self defense and on the owning and carrying of guns of any type, and gangs immediately lose their pool of helpless potential victims.

If they still manage to survive and still insist on killing one another, as long as they don't harm any innocents, society should stay out of their way. There is no cure for those who want to self destruct short of letting them do so while keeping innocents out of harm's way.

Gay Marriage

Government has no business being involved in marriage at all. Neither by "permitting" or licensing, or prohibiting it. Government involvement, of any sort, in marriage is a relatively new problem, and it is time to end it.

It does not harm any bystanders *at all* if two or more people of any gender decide to get married. Marriage should only be between the people involved, and the people they wish to include in their special day. If you think *your* marriage will somehow be "cheapened" or harmed by *someone else's* marriage, then your marriage is in serious trouble anyway.

For homosexual couples to ask for government to sanction their unions seems to be the case of people begging to give up some liberty so they can be just as violated as everyone else. Instead, heterosexuals should be demanding an end to government "recognition" of *their* unions.

Businesses should be free to recognize or offer services to any employee's family, based on any organizational plan, subject only to the owners' decisions.

Marriage should be a matter for the individuals involved, and *no one else*, to define.

Government Corruption

When you allow an organization to make, enforce, and interpret the rules it is expected to abide by, corruption is inevitable. When you allow that same organization to set the punishment for violations of those rules by those within its inner circle, the corruption is almost without risk.

The only way to end it is to disband the organization against that organization's wishes.

It might help if there were rules that could be enforced against the corrupt organization without relying on the organization's cooperation or consent, but this will never happen. That is what the US Constitution was *supposed* to do. Such dreams are Utopian and doomed to fail.

Corruption is an integral part of government and can never be eliminated from it. Imagining you can, by electing the "right people" or by "working within the system", is like taking a cube of ice out of your tea and imagining you can remove all the water from that ice cube, and still have regular ice.

Health Care

Socialists are partially right on health care. Health care *is* a right of each and every person. However, it is *not* an obligation of *anyone* to provide or finance health care for *anyone else*. No right places an *obligation* on anyone else beyond the obligation to *not violate* the exercise of that right.

You have the right to seek out any kind of health care you need or desire, *and* that you can *afford*. No one has an obligation to provide your health care for you, nor to pay your health care expenses.

They only have an obligation to not prevent you from seeking whatever health care you desire, and to not pass "laws" that seek to limit your options. This includes preventing you from obtaining and using any "drugs" or practices you feel may help, as long as you are harming no third person.

You have a right to *ask* others to help you pay for care you can't afford, but once you bring out the coercion and act as though your health care is an entitlement, don't expect sympathy.

Hunger

It is true that even in America there are people who don't have enough to eat. I have been there myself a time or two. Yet, we are all surrounded by edibles.

Silly "poaching laws" are one example of a rule that creates a problem where none would otherwise exist. Fortunately, most "country folk" ignore such "laws" when the need is real.

Often, cities and towns have "laws" regulating the appearance of property, as well as animal ordinances, which interfere with home food production.

Rules also strictly regulate the distribution of left-over food from restaurants and grocery stores. Much usable food goes to waste, because of fear of "arrest" or fines, even when the owners of the businesses in question would love to give it to those in need.

As with "drugs", people have a right to ingest anything they want, as long as they are not stealing it or using coercion in any way to obtain it, without anyone telling them otherwise.

You have a basic human right to eat, but no right *at all* to be fed.

Immigration

The "Border" is an imaginary line on a map drawn up by government. It has no basis in reality and is hurting individuals on both sides of the line, and *beyond*, by empowering government agents. Stop the insanity *now* and hope it isn't too late.

You have an absolute right to control who you allow on your property. However, you have no right *whatsoever* to control who your neighbor allows on *his* property. If your neighbor's guest leaves his property and steals from you or attacks you, you have a fundamental human right to defend yourself. It is the act of aggression that is the problem, not where the person committing the aggression came from.

All property should be privately owned. Look at any city park to see the "tragedy of the commons" illustrated in your own town. People take care of that which they own and trash that which they consider someone else's responsibility. Government can not legitimately own *anything* since it acquires nothing it did not steal from the original owner or purchase with money it took by force or threat of force. A thief does not own the stolen possessions he holds. Therefore government has no legitimate say in any trespassing dispute; only the real, individual owner of the property does. It doesn't matter where the trespasser originated. On private property a census worker is just as much a trespasser as an unofficial migrant from Mexico. And property without a real, individual *owner* can not be trespassed on.

Many people point to the existence and abuse of "social programs" as a reason to allow government to control immigration, but this only points out that socialism is unsustainable anywhere it is tried, and under whatever name you give it. It is essential that all welfare end, even the parts you personally approve of or benefit from. That a cure exposes another fatal disease that must also be dealt with doesn't discredit the cure. It just shows why liberty is not a piecemeal proposition.

As a humorous footnote, the people who are the strongest advocates of "immigration control" would find themselves in the position of having the founders of America, whom they claim to revere, *opposed* to their efforts.

In the Declaration of Independence, one of the enumerated grievances used as justification for secession from Great Britain was immigration control: "*He has endeavoured to prevent the population of these States; for that purpose obstructing the Laws for Naturalization of Foreigners; refusing to pass others to encourage their migrations hither...*" (emphasis mine)

Wave *that* in some Tea Partier's face!

Inflation

When people notice that it takes more money to purchase the same things *now* than it did a year ago, they often blame the price increase on the "greedy business" or on unions. That is rarely the truth of the matter.

Instead, "inflation" is what happens when the money in your pocket has been devalued by the organization which issues the money.

When the "Federal Reserve Bank" (which is *not* "federal", has *no* "reserves", and *is not* a "bank") prints more money, each dollar it prints makes the dollar in your pocket or in your bank account lose just a little more of its value. Over time this adds up, or subtracts *down*, as the case may be.

The prices are not going *up*, the value of your money is going *down*.

This is possible because most governments prefer to issue fiat money, which is not backed by anything other than the groundless belief that it has value simply because the government *says* it has value.

Fiat money always *always* *ALWAYS* eventually fails. However, those with government connections, who will get the newly created "dollars" hot off the press or with the stroke of a computer key, profit greatly from this counterfeiting racket. They get to use the new dollars before their creation has damaged the value of all the dollars in circulation.

This is why, until people stop accepting the phony money, governments will continue the scam. Until you put an end to it, they can keep getting away with causing and *profiting from* inflation while you work harder and harder for less and less real wealth.

Once inflation starts in earnest, immediately stop accepting government fiat money as payment for *anything*. Not for wages or as payment for items you sell. Only accept gold, silver, food, or durable goods which you can use or trade for things you will need later. If you don't you will lose out.

In fact, it would not hurt you to start getting some practice using *real* money now, before it becomes necessary.

Infrastructure

This falls under the topic of "**Big Projects**" and is also covered under "**Free Riders**".

We have government *now*, yet America's infrastructure is crumbling and failing. This is *killing* innocent people.

There *is* a better way, and it doesn't rely on coercion and theft.

Let individuals and businesses pay for, build, and *own* the bridges, roads, airports, sewer systems, generators, power grid, and reservoirs they want.

Let them take the risks and reap the benefits. Let them find solutions that were never permitted or explored before.

Jurors

Jurors are the last line of defense against tyranny before weapons are necessary.

Regardless of the instructions a judge may issue, a juror has the right, and the *obligation*, to judge *not only* if the accused has violated the "law" as charged, but also whether the "law" is right or wrong.

If the "law" attempts to control, prohibit, or regulate *anything* other than actual aggression (a physical attack on an innocent person), theft, fraud, or trespass on privately-owned property, then the "law" is not legitimate (it is a *counterfeit* "law") and it is the duty and responsibility of the juror to find the accused "not guilty" regardless of whether the person committed the act they are on trial for or not.

It is critical that good people who understand the power of a juror get seated on every single jury to rescue people from bad "laws" and overzealous enforcers.

Educate yourself and *become* of of those good people. Please find the nearest branch of the Fully Informed Jury Association (www.fija.org) and help them get the word out to all potential jurors while you still can.

Justice System

"Justice" is what we call the attempt to take an individual who has been harmed and correct the damage.

Justice is only complete when the victim is returned to the condition they were in before the harm occurred.

It has *nothing* to do with punishment or revenge except in the sick minds of statists.

As long as a government is in control of, in fact *owns*, the courts, there can be *no* justice. It just isn't in the equation.

"Fines" are paid by those found guilty, but the money goes mainly to the government itself, unlike restitution. It rarely helps the damaged individuals at all.

In cases where the government is one of the involved parties, it is especially dishonest to allow the government court to control any part of the process. As a first step toward justice, government must bow out of any court case where it is either the "aggrieved" party or the accused party. Let a disinterested third party adjudicate instead. At least until we can get a true separation of court and State, and start serving *real* justice.

Liability

If you cause harm to an innocent individual through your actions, whether harm was intentional or not, you are liable for restitution.

In a free society you would not be able to hide behind a title, badge, political office, corporation, or desk. Actions have consequences and consequences can have costs.

Whether you cause $1.98 worth of damage, or 200 billion dollars worth of damage, you are liable for that full amount. *Personally.* A person may be willing to forgive part or all of your debt to them, but you have no right or authority to demand they accept less than you owe.

If you initiate force against (attack) or coerce a person, the consequence could mean they strike back with self-defensive violence. And that would be completely within their rights no matter what reason you give, what excuse you think you have, or what your job may be.

Current politicians and enforcers would either change their ways in a free society or be eliminated quickly. There would be no "slap on the wrist" followed by an announcement that "*they acted according to departmental guidelines*".

Middle East

Regardless of your opinions, unless you *live* there the troubles in the Middle East are none of your business. Unless they come and attack you when you did *not* attack, or meddle in their affairs, *first*. All sides in the Middle East conflict, and *especially* their governments, are committing atrocities, and are not worthy of your support.

To "tax" people and use that stolen money to send troops in other people's names to meddle in the affairs of others is wrong.

If you wish to pay your own way (or get someone to *voluntarily* pay your way), you are free to travel anywhere in the world and fight for any cause you support. Attack the innocent and you are the guilty one, you deserve no mercy, and you are *not* a hero.

Entangling alliances abroad lead to tragedy and terrorism at home. There should be no official support, or economic or military meddling, anywhere in the world.

Military

The people who founded America did not want a "standing army" (a full-time military that still existed even when America is not being attacked and invaded).

The founders understood the danger of establishing a class of people who would become reliant on continuing military threats. They also understood that a standing military too easily becomes the personal tool of a tyrant, to be used to advance his agenda at home or overseas.

This is one reason they wrote the Second Amendment and attempted to protect the right of you and me to own and to carry, anywhere we went, any type of weapon we desired, in any way we wished, without asking permission of anyone, ever. They intended for you and me to have firearms of the current military pattern and function, which today means *fully-automatic machine guns*, with which to defend our homes and our towns from *all* aggressors, *especially* from any government agents, employees, or politicians who might try to usurp our individual sovereignty.

Professional militaries depend for their livelihood upon keeping a continuous threat and active enemies. It is not in their self-interest to have peace. No *threat* means no *job*.

Instead, America was established to depend on a *militia* for defense. The militia is *you* and it is *me*. We are responsible for our own defense.

All the weapons of the military belong in our hands; not in the hands of megalomaniacal officers or politicians.

For the "big stuff", like tanks, fighter jets, and nuclear missiles, they have proven to be less effective in the 21st century than guerrilla fighters. People defending their homes have an advantage over invaders, even invaders with expensive tools.

However, there will always be wealthy people who can afford to finance these expensive weapons, or finance ways to make the big things obsolete. And there will never be a shortage of people who get their only self-worth from self-identifying as a "warrior" and will thus volunteer to train to use the big weapons.

A government-owned military is a danger to liberty. I know some of those in the government's military really *think* they are doing good. Instead, they are being used as pawns by a government that only cares about them as long as it *needs* them.

They are brainwashed into thinking they are "fighting for our freedom" when they are most demonstrably *not*.

Their presence and actions around the world are causing America to be *much less* free and safe: they are creating new generations of people who hate America and are willing to die in order to strike back however they can.

If the injured people in these other countries would blame the *US government*, which is the real aggressor, it would be fine, but it is easier to blame American individuals *instead* (many *Americans* make a similar error).

The government officials usually have heavy protection wherever they go, unlike the average American at home or overseas, so guess who is the easier target. Remember, too, that it isn't "terrorism" if it targets a government facility or employee, but only if it targets *private* individuals, regardless of the self-serving claims of the statists.

There is another problem which has the potential to become even worse. Too many ex-military folk are now going into "law-enforcement" when they get discharged; using their military training and "*us* vs. *them*" attitude against Americans in their own towns. Once you work for The State, and advance its agenda with force elsewhere, you have an easier time doing the same against people at home whom The State tells you are *also* "your enemy".

The police have *become* the standing army *among us* that the founders warned against permitting.

Frequently, the "enemies" The State sends these militarized enforcers to kidnap or kill have done *nothing* against anyone else, but are only asserting their rights to ingest anything they wish, to protect their property rights, to engage in free trade, or to own and to carry any type of weapon they want, everywhere they go, in any manner they see fit, without asking permission from anyone, *ever*. In other words, for exercising the exact thing these ex-military folks *claimed* to be fighting for all along: **freedom**.

I expect that if any military supporters read this, they will tear me apart for being "anti-military". I am not anti-military since I fully support the militia; I just don't confuse the *legitimate* military with the pawns of The State. Do *you*?

Money

"Money" is anything that is used as a placeholder for things you want. A few people actually want the money *itself*, which is fine, but most of us want what we can trade the money to get.

"Money" can be gold, silver, chocolate, seashells, or anything you can convince others to take in trade. It doesn't need to be rare or "valuable", although it *helps* if it can't be found covering the ground or growing on trees all around the person you are trying to convince to take it in trade. If it is that common, then it will probably take a lot more of it to balance the trade (this is known as "inflation"), and that makes it more difficult to carry and deliver. It is also nice if your money doesn't rot quickly. Being "rich" in crated bananas would be a very transitory wealth.

Government "money" satisfies some of the criteria to be good money, but it fails miserably on others. Those failures are more than sufficient to invalidate government money completely and to show the superiority of free-market money.

Money should never be *forced* on someone. No one should dictate what you "should" use as your money, nor should they limit you to one type of money. Let the market choose the money that people trust and want. Even if that means some would choose to accept printed paper IOUs backed by nothing but a promise from a group of thieves that the money is "good", that is their choice. In this case, "*seller* beware!"

This is why it is a bad idea to have one person or one organization in control of all the money for a particular region. It is too easy for them to manipulate the money supply to enrich themselves at the expense of everyone else. When you allow them to have the power of government monopolistic coercion backing them up you are begging for disaster. Even if the people in charge of the money were "good people", infinitely more honest than the average person on Earth, the temptation is too great. That kind of power always attracts power-hungry bad people. Of all the people or groups to give a monopoly over the power to create "money", government is the absolute *worst*.

Personally, I prefer trading for silver or gold for most exchanges. Sometimes, if I am in need of something that another person has an excess of, we can work out a satisfactory deal based on *that* alternative currency. That is as it should be and how money should be allowed to work.

Morality

Morality changes depending on the dominant culture. Of course, that dominant culture will deny this fact *vehemently* saying that this is "moral relativism" and is "immoral".

Today, in America, it would be "immoral" for a 30 year-old man to marry a 13 year-old woman, but in colonial America, that would have been perfectly "moral".

It isn't that the act was once "right" and then became "wrong", it is that the opinions of the dominant culture changed.

Right and wrong, on the other hand, are *not* dependent on the majority opinion, but are objective and do not change without a foundational change in reality.

Killing someone *except* in self defense or defense of property is wrong. Stealing is wrong. Kidnapping, rape, defrauding- all are acts that are wrong everywhere for all times. It does not matter if you are a farmer or a cop; the job title does not change the wrongness.

Religious ideas, a prime example of morality, may be congruent with right and wrong, or they may be completely counter to the concepts. In many cases, a religion may advocate harming an individual who is harming no one in any way, just because he is violating some rule the religion dictates. To the followers of that religion, his actions are "immoral" and justify the harm that is then done to him. To those who *do not* follow that particular religion, the harm done to the "sinner" is immoral and wrong.

This illustrates why "morality" is no measure of right or wrong.

There is *right* and there is *wrong*. Harming someone who does not deserve to be harmed right now (due to them currently *not* being involved in initiating force or fraud) is *wrong*, regardless of the culture. Morality is not as clear. Morality is a poor substitute for ethics and principles.

National Defense

"Defense" is standing your ground against an attack on your own person or territory. It is *not "fight them over there so you don't have to fight them over here"*. That is an **invasion**, which is *offense*. It makes *you* the aggressor and makes you *wrong*.

It also accomplishes the opposite of what its proponents claim. It makes your home territory much *less* safe as it gives other ethically-challenged people the justification they might want to "fight us over *here* so they don't have to fight us over *there*" in *their* own homes.

Trade with *all* nations; entangling alliances with *none*. It's the *sensible* course. You may have also noticed it is never the course taken as long as government sets policy. Government will never choose the sensible course, which is why we must form a free society in order to be smart and right about true defense.

National Parks/Forests/Monuments

All property should be privately owned. Government can not really own *anything*, since everything it possesses it stole or "bought" with stolen (or counterfeited) money. A thief can not rightfully control the stolen property which he possesses.

Property that is privately owned is normally cared for more conscientiously than property that is "public". If you have spent much time in "national parks" or "national forests", "behind the curtain", away from the corridors the casual visitors travel, you will have seen the misuse of the environment that government "ownership" has wrought.

It wouldn't take much effort to care for the natural environment better, while charging a visitor's fee for use of the lands. Some people balk at the thought of *paying* to travel into areas that were once "national". You already *do*. You are "taxed" and then charged *more* if you wish to actually use that which you supposedly own a share of.

Visit a few privately-owned camp grounds or attractions and compare them to government-controlled camp grounds or tourist destinations and see the possibilities that true pride of ownership can bring.

Pirates

Theft is theft, and aggression is aggression. There is no type that is "better" or "worse" than any other. In many cases pirates only do, *without* government backing, the exact same things government navies and coast guards do. If it is wrong for pirates to do, then it is wrong for government employees to do.

However, piracy has a solution, and the solution is known and hasn't changed in hundreds of years.

First of all, stop trespassing along the coasts of places where you are not wanted. This simple step would end much piracy immediately.

Secondly, stop disarming the crews and passengers of all commercial ships and recreational boats. Pirates, like *all* aggressors, prefer unarmed targets. Stop handing thieves and aggressors what they want. How difficult is that to grasp?

What if a port of call doesn't allow guns? If peaceable *armed* people are not welcome in some "territorial waters" or ports, then you are not really welcome there *at all*. Avoid these enemies and trade only with people who *respect* your rights. Is your life really worth so little you would risk it to make an enemy more comfortable?

Poaching

Added to The State's list of prohibited victimless acts is the imaginary offense of "poaching".

"Poaching" is the act of not recognizing government's claim over something it does not own: the wildlife that lives within the government's imaginary borders.

I suppose it is not *surprising* that the government employees claim they own the deer, since they also behave as though they own the *humans*, but it is a concept I will continue to correct when I run across it.

Purchasing a license from the government in order to hunt is admitting that you agree that government owns the animals. It doesn't.

Poaching would only be wrong if someone owns the wild animals which are running free, or if you trespassed to get to the animals. No one owns the animals in most cases, since The State can own nothing it did not first steal, and thieves have no authority to dictate what can be done with the property they stole.

You should obviously ask a property owner before hunting on his land, but if a deer is on *your* property, and it has no ownership indicators, such as a collar or a tag, it is yours to take. If the animal is on your property and it *is* identified as someone's animal, then its owner owes you restitution for any damage it does while on your property.

Hunting is an activity that teaches people to provide for themselves. It short-circuits the welfare cycle that government depends upon for dependence and loyalty.

Pretending to own the wildlife and then selling permission to hunt it simply gives The State more unwarranted power over the people. It is another way to take money from productive people and give it to the parasites of government.

Plus, in order to hunt, people need to own effective weapons and have the skills to use them. That is more reason for government to demand a hunting license: to keep track of armed people.

Hunting often involves tracking and stalking and an awareness of your surroundings. Those are skills that your enemies would not like for you to hone, since they may serve you in the future.

I am certainly not advocating mindless slaughter of wildlife. I *hate* waste. I would not shoot it unless I was prepared to eat it, or otherwise use it.

I also know that some of the money from licenses

goes toward habitat and such, but the amount is a tiny percentage (that which is left over after the excessive bureaucracy is paid for) and could be done much better by the market through privately owned property. Mostly your license fees go to support those who want to exercise control over you and your guns.

Don't undercut freedom by supporting The State with your obedience or with your money. You owe The State nothing.

Police

Civilization got along just fine *without* police for thousands of years- until the middle of the 19th century; it can (and *will*) get along just fine without them again.

In fact, the mere existence of police *causes* crime. This is just based upon what I observe about human behavior, but it holds up to scrutiny. I'm not even talking about all the murderers, thieves, and rapists who wear badges, or the crimes against humanity committed "in the line of duty" due to enforcement of counterfeit "laws"; I am talking about free-lance theft, murder, rape, and whatever else falls under the label of *real* crime. (Nor am I talking about the peaceful, consensual, victimless, yet "illegal", behavior of others who are harming no innocent person, since those things are only "crimes" to The State, but not to *sensible* people.)

I have witnessed what happens when someone stumbles. If they are with one person, that person will normally try to catch them before they fall. If the stumbler is with a couple of people, though, often they will fall before either of the people act. They each thought the *other* person would grab the tripping friend. It isn't a purposeful desire to watch someone fall, but is just a result of not acting because there is a question of whether someone else will take care of the situation. Even a slight hesitation is too much. I think the same principle applies to crime.

Crime thrives where people believe it is someone else's responsibility to take action. In big cities it is easy to think someone else will get involved, so you will "mind your own business" while theft and aggression continues.

This is even more true where there are a lot of cops. If someone is supposedly being *paid* to stop crime, it is even easier to turn away and let them "handle it".

In fact, cops actively encourage this irresponsible behavior by criminalizing and punishing self-defense. "Don't be a hero," they say. "Call the professionals." Except that cops are under *no legal obligation* to protect you, as an *individual*, from crime. Try to sue the local LEOs after they fail to protect you from crime if you doubt me.

Stop contributing to the success of crime. Ignore the cops and take responsibility for your *own* safety. If it is in your nature, take responsibility for the safety of those around you. Don't wait for some "professional", whose priorities are not where you may assume they are, to step up and fix it for you.

Pollution

Air pollution and water pollution are particularly difficult to fight under the current system.

Because no one owns the atmosphere, the rivers, or the oceans, no one can effectively seek restitution when they have been harmed by the irresponsible polluting of another.

There is also the problem that in many cases, since government lays claim to the atmosphere and waters, the polluter will pay a "fine" to the government and be off the hook. Often while the polluting *continues*. In some cases it is cheaper to keep paying fines than to stop polluting. This is obviously to the detriment of those actually harmed.

When *government* is the guilty party, actual restitution is even *more* difficult to collect.

Because of property rights, you have a right to pollute your own property as much as you want, in any way you want. You may make your property worthless and make a future sale for a decent price highly unlikely, but those are some of the consequences and that is your choice to make.

However, once your pollution leaves your property- on the wind, through groundwater, in a river, by radiating, by rolling down hill, or on the backs of turtles- you have damaged the property of another and you owe them for those damages.

There is *always* a way to keep your filth to yourself, without allowing it to harm others, even if you think it is too expensive. It is just a cost of producing damaging by-products. If you are smart, you may find a market for those by-products and make a profit from them as well, rather than letting them go to waste, but that's another issue.

In a free society, there would probably arise pollution detectives who would track down the source of any pollutant you might be suffering, for a fee. Once the source is found, negotiations leading to restitution, shunning, or self defense (depending on the circumstances and the cooperation of the polluter) could begin to set things right.

Pornography/Child Pornography

In the case of fully self-responsible individuals, as long as no one was coerced into posing for photographs or performing on video, no harm was committed. Not even if it offends you. And cartoon-type materials, which show *no actual people* (yet can be punished just the same under the current system), *can not* be harming *anyone*.

Viewing pornography does not lead to sexual assaults, and this has been shown to be true time after time, all over the world. Instead it is a safe outlet for people who might otherwise be frustrated into attacking someone. Frustration is no justification, of course, no matter how intense.

So, moving right along to the case of people who for reasons of maturity or mental ability are *not* fully self-responsible...

This is a subject more personally dangerous to mention, and more divisive, than "abortion". It is "*child* pornography".

Almost everyone wants to protect innocent children. It is in our nature.

Some people, though, have a *broken* nature and want to prey on the innocent. Many of these find jobs with government where they can cause harm with no fear of breaking the "law". Others (we will pretend the categories don't overlap) exploit innocent children sexually.

I often find myself taking the hated position of attempting to point out that just because the agents of The State kidnap someone on charges of possessing child pornography, it doesn't mean the person did anything wrong, or even actually had any of the forbidden materials in their possession.

I suspect it is very easy to plant such images in a person's computer in order to be able to lock them up without anyone speaking out in their defense. It has become our modern "witchcraft" accusation; impossible to survive once made. Don't think the goons of The State don't recognize and take advantage of this fact.

"Child pornography" even includes what I consider the "Stephen King-ish victims". Should Stephen King be on death row for all the murders and atrocities he has "committed" in his books? Of course not. Why should an equivalent creative act that involves no real victims (no matter how revolting it is to most of us) be punished?

Cartoon characters which *could* be interpreted to be imaginary children are not harmed no matter what anyone does to them. If the majority of studies are correct, this type of "child pornography" could actually *prevent* real attacks on actual innocent children, rather than "inspiring" them as the detractors claim. Regardless: no victim; no aggression.

When a child victim of pornographic exploitation grows to be a responsible self-owning person, he or she should have total control over what is done with the images of their child self, including getting all copies away from the feds' "child porn database" (for "research"... riiiight...). Even if we don't like what they choose to do with their personal property, such as publishing it for others to view. Otherwise you are telling them they do not own themselves, but the collective- *"society"*- does. That is wrong and harmful, and two wrongs don't make a right.

It is also dangerous to point out that most teenagers are *not* "children" even if The State declares them so.

Some may *not* yet be fully responsible for themselves and some undoubtedly *are*. Chronological age has no bearing on this; responsibility, acceptance of the consequences, and self-ownership *do*. To make a "one-size-punishes-all" law harms everyone in the long run. This is the absurdity of the "sexting crisis".

Society and The State's prosecutors do not own the person's body and have no authority over what is done with images of it.

Since I know I will be misrepresented, it is probably pointless to state this, but I will anyway: I don't want to view any child pornography. I don't understand its attraction to some; I would violently defend *any* child who was being exploited in this way whether they were familiar to me or not.

If I knew someone who had an attraction to child pornography, I would keep my children away from him and would warn everyone I knew to watch him near their kids. I would *NOT* tattle to The State, however.

I would also try to remember that all is not as it seems when The State wants to get rid of someone. Governments *lie*. It is what they do best, except for stealing, kidnapping, and killing, that is.

Poverty

Long before government tried to corner the market in taking care of the poor, it was a task willingly accepted by charities. And, charities did very *well* at it.

Poverty, in a great many cases, is a government-caused, or exacerbated, problem. Plus, the government's "solutions" make it harder and harder to escape.

There would be no real problem with having no money in a *free* society. You could trade or work for your homestead, grow or trade for your food, raise your own livestock for food and clothes, and seek the kind of medical services and products you could afford. If you decided you needed *money* for something, since it is a very useful thing to have on occasion, it would be easy to find a way to earn some.

You could start a business from your own home, doing or making anything you think others might pay you to do or make. You could run your business for a few weeks, or for years, depending on what you wanted to do, and how much money you needed.

The problems arise when government steps in.

It has been made *illegal* to be poor. You must pay property taxes, either directly or added to the price of your rent, or you will be homeless.

Barter is seen as "avoiding taxation".

Almost every normal human activity is subject to a government fee, for which government fiat money is the required payment.

Government's rules complicate the earning of money beyond reason.

It has become very difficult to start a business (or take over an established one) because of the huge burden of red tape, regulations, licenses, fees, permits, inspections... all manifestations of government.

Even if you manage to have a little money on hand, government adds to the cost of *everything* you do or buy in countless ways. Every single thing you buy is made more expensive with taxes added at every stage of production. Many things are either heavily regulated or prohibited, both of which inflate the price artificially.

Government demands money from each of us all the time (including those who are out there producing what *we* really want and need to purchase) for the provision all the unwanted and burdensome "services" we are forced to accept.

This also adds to the cost of production. Each of these costs only add to the problem of poverty.

The solution to poverty is to get government out of the way of those who want to make their own way in the world.

Stop prohibiting entrepreneurs from finding their own innovative solutions, and allow them to hire whoever they need.

Stop allowing government to keep a hand in the cookie jar of each and every business; adding to the cost of production until we all end up having 7/8 of our production go toward supporting government at all levels. That's a form of welfare none of us can afford to support.

Let charities pick up the slack for those who need temporary or permanent assistance, and let people escape the welfare cycle.

Prisons/ Prison overcrowding

Prison is a cage. It does *nothing* to help the people who have been victimized by aggressors. It does *nothing* to restore stolen property to the victims of theft. Prison doesn't even stop the bad guys from doing bad things to innocent people.

What it *does* do is create a bonding experience for those imprisoned. It reinforces the "*us* vs. *them*" mentality. It is creating a subculture that is bad for society.

It also puts honest and non-aggressive people, who are held captive for violating some *counterfeit* "law", in a closed society with people who think nothing of attacking, stealing, and defrauding others as a way of life. It is a university where real bad guys are teaching *non-aggressive* people aggression and thieving skills.

Prisons are expensive to build, run, and maintain, and they are almost all over-crowded. This is ridiculous. There is no reason for prisons to be overcrowded.

Most of the people in prison have done nothing *wrong.* They have *harmed* no other person. They are political prisoners who are only caged because they did something government decided to prohibit. Something like keeping and bearing arms, ingesting a chemical or plant, consensual sex, not cooperating with thieves, being poor, not asking permission for using their own property, etc.

People who have harmed no innocent person should be left alone to live their lives as they see fit. Even if it means they harm themselves or offend you with their actions.

Let the justice system focus on those who have actually caused physical or financial harm to others. Instead of prison, any *real* justice system needs to focus on restitution. Anything less is not "justice" and only adds to the harm.

Property Rights

Having property rights means that if you own something, you have the right to use that thing in any way you wish, as long as by doing so you do not initiate force and thereby violate another person's rights to "life, liberty, and property".

Governments never truly respect any property rights but their own, which ironically don't really *exist* since there is no individual who holds the rights over the property that government claims; along with the fact that government possesses *nothing* which it did not steal or "buy" with stolen or counterfeited "money". Stolen property does not belong to the thief who possesses it. Just to be clear: ***Government has no property rights***.

There are three types of property rights that I can see. There are property rights over **your body**, which for the purposes of this discussion I will call *"bodily property rights"* (otherwise known as "self-ownership"). There are property rights over the **stuff you own**, such as your cars, guns, boots, knick-knacks, appliances, and skull collection. I'll call this your *"stuff rights"*. Then, there are property rights over your **real estate**- property such as your land, home, or business location, which I'll call your *"real estate rights"*.

Starting with your **bodily property rights**: Take your *living body* out of the equation and the other two types of property rights vanish (along with all your other rights) except when they transfer to *someone else*. This means that your existence brings into being your "bodily property rights". Your rights to own, use, and destroy your **stuff** and your **real estate** derive from your existence.

If one thing (such as a right) brings forth another thing, then the *fundamental* thing outranks that which derives from it. That means that your "bodily property rights", from which your "stuff rights" and your "real estate rights" come, must *necessarily* come before any other property rights if we are to be consistent. After all, you can't have a hangnail if you have no hands or feet.

Now, what about a property owner's "real estate rights" trumping a customer/employee/visitor's *bodily* property rights? If you invite someone, can you *really* demand they leave their bodily property rights behind? Is that even a real *invitation*? Is such a demand valid? Does such a demand violate a person's rights by initiating a kind of force? Can you attack them simply because you claim that is a condition of them coming onto your property? Is slavery "OK" as long as you only do it on your own property? Do you own the space between the visitor's skin and their clothing when they enter your property so that you can dictate what resides there? Does the ownership of that space change as a person travels from place to place throughout the day? When you really consider that concept, the absurdity becomes apparent.

I *know* I have no claim on your "bubble" of bodily personal property no matter what I might prefer, nor upon anything that may be there as long as it doesn't make an appearance on my property. Be warned that others may disagree and lay claim upon your body, your clothing, and the space that exists between the two. That doesn't mean they are right.

I think that the position that "real estate rights" trump the "bodily property rights" and the "stuff rights" of anyone invited to enter the real estate comes from a real desire to be nice and respectful to the real estate's owner. That is fine. It is not always the wisest thing to exercise every right you possess at every moment. I do think it is putting the cart before the horse, though. Perhaps people are afraid of the reaction the general public might have if this realization were to become common.

Property rights are *almost* sacred, but they *do* have a limit: **They end where the property ends**. That is not really a limit, it is just a recognition that there can be no overlap.

I have an absolute right to forbid access by anyone to my property. Once I decide to allow people to come onto my property, there are limits to what I can do to my visitors. They do not become my property once they step across my "border".

If I own a business where I invite the general public (in other words "*all individuals who are not currently engaged in aggression*"), or if I invite a person into my home, I recognize that I have no right to demand to control what objects are inside their clothing or what thoughts are inside their minds. They do not become part of my property when they accept my invitation to come onto my property. My property rights extend to the surface of their clothing or their exposed skin and no farther.

I am "adult enough" to know where my property ends and theirs begins. I can not *demand* that they carry a gun for self-defense even though it would increase the level of safety on my property if they *did*. I can't search them for "drugs". I can not demand that they believe the same way I do about state aggression and liberty. As long as it isn't leaking beyond the confines of their "bubble of personal property" I can't demand that they not carry plutonium or anthrax.

If they begin "leaking" radiation, spores, racial epithets, aggression, or bullets I can take whatever steps I deem necessary to protect my property, since those things, having left the *visitor's* personal property, are now trespassing (if unwelcome) on *my* property.

Race Relations

A racist is someone, *anyone*, who makes an issue of race. Authoritarianism, whether of the "left" or "right", is often racist. It depends on the tactic of "divide and conquer", and "race" is a convenient divider.

Libertarianism, on the other hand, is an open door, open to *all* who do not attack or defraud others, regardless of anything else. Even if they have bad thoughts.

Everyone has a "right to be wrong" in how they think. That is not the issue. The issue is when you begin taking actions which harm the innocent based on those wrong ideas.

Racism is wrong. Treating someone as a second-class person because of their race is wrong. Giving anyone "special perks" based on their race is wrong. Making an issue of race *at all* is ridiculous; just as it is to make an issue of gender or sexual orientation, or which side of an imaginary "national border" you were born on.

Based as it is on absolute self-ownership and non-aggression, libertarianism can not act in racist ways without violating its own core values. You can't be fighting for freedom if you are making an issue of someone's race.

Authoritarianism, however, based as it is on a small group controlling the rest of society, thrives on racism. It helps to keep people angry, resentful, suspicious, and hateful if you want to be able to pass endless laws against the "others" of either side. Therefore The State and its supporters endlessly fan the flames of racism, seeing it everywhere except in their own behavior.

Don't empower authoritarians by falling for this trick. Judge people on their actions. That is what counts, not silly things like how much melanin is in the outer layers of their skin. If you want to hate me, hate me for the choices I make and the ideas I hold, not my genetic makeup.

Everyone has the right to associate with whoever they want for any reason. It is not within governmental authority to control this. Personal responsibility and Darwinian selection will be much more effective in the long run, anyway.

Don't expect others to treat you fairly or rise to defend you if you are hateful to any particular genetic group.

The right of association means that anyone can choose who they associate with or do business with. If someone is discriminating based upon race (or anything else as silly) then this person can be shunned by others who think he is wrong. No need for government *or* coercion.

Religion

Any government strong enough to endorse or promote your religion is also strong enough to prohibit your religion when the climate becomes less friendly.

I know there are a lot of people who are afraid of Muslims taking over America. I know because I hear from them all the time.

I wouldn't like that outcome any more than anyone else would, but I also don't think Islam is the only religious threat to freedom. It seems to me that liberty is caught in a continuing repeat of the Crusades, even now in the 21st Century. Truthfully I don't want *either* side to win.

A great many of the very people so worried about this *now* ignored and encouraged previous violations of the separation of church and state and made such a scenario possible. By insisting on violating the freedom of religion of others, they *built* the tool and are now fearful of that tool being turned against them.

Believe anything you want to believe. Don't try to force me to pretend to agree with you. Once you do, you make defensive action against you a legitimate choice. It doesn't matter which version of god you are pushing. It doesn't matter if you are trying to impose Sharia "law" on the non-Muslim or trying to use stolen money to pay for monuments to the Judeo-Christian Ten Commandments to be put in government courthouses.

Religion has no business being the basis of *any* rule that is applied to those who do not follow that particular religion. What is "moral" to one religion is "an abomination" to another.

Stick with the few rules that predate and transcend religion: Don't initiate force (or *accept* initiated force), and don't initiate deception.

Freedom of religion *must* include freedom *from* religion if it is to have any meaning whatsoever. However, this only means no one has a right to force their religion on you, individually or by "law". Being exposed to a religion is not the same as having it forced upon you. Seeing a person praying, or a Christmas display, or any other sort of religious ritual does not harm you.

People have an individual right to believe anything they want to believe, even if it is *wrong*. That includes all religions- his, hers, mine, and yours.

Retirement

Would you really *choose* to depend on someone else to support you in your old age? What if it were someone who had *lied* to you throughout your entire life about one thing after another? What if it were someone who only valued you for what they could get from you? Someone like a government.

Don't depend on government retirement plans such as "Social Security" being there, or being adequate, when needed.

You know your own needs better than any one else, *especially* some bureaucrat, ever could. You could invest your money more wisely, too. If only you were permitted to keep all you earn, instead of having around 87% of your total production end up going to government in some fashion.

Let people prepare for their own future, with everything they have produced with the labor of their own body available for the purpose. If they don't trust themselves to provide for a good retirement, allow them to voluntarily contract with someone they *do* trust. End the coercive practices government currently imposes.

"Rich Warlord"

One of the main excuses that cause people to cling to the archaic notion of government is a fear of the "rich warlord" who would supposedly take over your life, without repercussions, if no government were holding him back. It is claimed that government is the only thing that keeps such a villain contained or from gaining power.

Let's examine this idea.

Would people who have tasted real liberty be so easy to take it from again? Probably not for a generation or two. Plus, in a *free* society they would have acquired the proper tools with which to fend off bad guys more effectively.

However, there would undoubtedly come a time when the lure of ease and "safety" would sound nice to the less honorable among us. Then the cycle would start anew. Someone would propose the idea of setting up another government "for the common good", and *foolishly*, many would go along.

Even so, I think it is better to start from scratch occasionally than to watch The State get bigger, more tyrannical, and less benevolent while doing nothing to stop it.

Even if a new government being created is inevitable, which I am *not* convinced of, I think it is good to make them rebuild The State from the ground up ever so often. If you can't dig up the weed, at least chop it off at ground level from time to time.

But considering the "warlord" again: First of all, would this really be worse than the situation we are in now?

We already live under a rich warlord who steals over 87% of our economic production, and demands more of your money and more control over your life every year. He will kill us if we refuse to pay. He demands a ransom be paid on our homes or he will steal them from us, and kill us if we resist. He demands control over whether or not we are allowed to own and carry effective weapons of self defense, and has criminalized the most effective ones; the very ones his own Constitution puts off-limits for him to regulate *in any way*. He demands control over our travel, our business, our children, even our own bodies. He pretends to be a benevolent protector, and seems honestly bewildered at those of us who see through his velvety smooth words to the harsh truth behind them.

This rich warlord is the main proponent of the phantom boogeyman of the other, *unknown*, rich warlord.

Perhaps the monster we *don't* know really *is* worse than the monster we *know*. What then?

I think that the only time to keep the rich warlord from becoming a real problem is before he consolidates his power, amasses an army, and passes "laws" that make it hard, or even impossible, to stop him. In other words, kill him upon his first act of aggression.

Do you think he will behave nicely his whole life until one day he suddenly starts acting like the blossoming monster he is to become? I would imagine he will have a life-long history of aggression and coercion. Remove the "legal" prohibitions on self-defense and he will not survive to become a real threat.

This means we are already at an extremely difficult phase in trying to rein in the full grown monster we currently know. Not impossible, but it will take a paradigm shift where enough people realize it is necessary. What is the tipping point?

Roads

I am frequently asked how we will have roads if there are no government road programs or fuel taxes. This ignores the historical fact that roads existed long before governments ever declared ownership over them.

All roads should be privatized. Everyone would own the road that runs through their property. Or if it runs along a boundary, they would own the road up to their property lines, perhaps right down the center line.

Now, if I owned half of the road in front of my property, would I want the bother of maintaining it, and the liability if someone was driving on it and was in an accident? No, I wouldn't. Would this mean I would close off the road to travelers? *I* wouldn't, but I am sure some folks would.

Would there be any profit in keeping the road open? Yes. But no one, including me, wants a toll-booth every hundred feet or so. So what would happen? I think that the market would soon find a workable solution.

My hunch is that companies would form which would buy or lease roads from land-owners (or possibly just take over the management of the roads), taking on all costs and liabilities, but also

125

most of the profits.

These companies (not "corporations", which are a government creation) would probably sell a form of travel insurance (or something of the sort) that would permit travel upon their roadways and also guarantee against road hazards, and maybe even mechanical problems. They could also sell, lease, or manage business locations along the shoulders.

That is only the beginning. What would stop inventors from creating vehicles that don't even *need* smoothly maintained roads? They could be a new type of "off-road" or flying vehicles. The biggest stumbling block along this line has been (for over 50 years) the government regulations which cripple innovation. Does the FAA sound familiar?

So you will have a choice: use the roads and pay a fee which would undoubtedly be less than the fuel taxes you pay now, or leave the surface entirely.

Sex

Consensual sex between *responsible individuals* is none of my business, nor is it any of your business. *Unless* someone involved chooses to *make* it your business, but even in that case, you have no authority to enforce your moral code on other people, nor to decide for someone else whether they are "responsible enough". I can't understand the notion that sex is fair game for government busy-bodies to pry into. If you wish to rent or trade your sexual favors, as long as you are under no "monogamy contract" or other sort of voluntary exclusivity agreement, that is *your* business (literally).

Consent is the key. Silence is *not* "consent". In order to consent, there must be no coercion and all participating individuals must actually agree to the activity.

If you are the recipient of unwanted sexual advances, say "no". As long as it stops there, there is no need to get violent or hateful. Forced sex is never right and you have every right to defend yourself against it with as much force as it takes to stop the threat.

"Age of consent" is strictly a governmental notion which, in America, has fluctuated wildly between 10 and 18 years of age, depending on the era. One size does not fit all, because biology is *not* constrained by "law". Sexual activity *IS* constrained by biology, however, so pre-pubescent children are *always* off-limits.

Most people are decent, and whether they are homosexual, heterosexual, bisexual, polyamorous, or asexual does not change that fact.

Discrimination based on a person's sex life is stupid and wrong, but there should not be "laws" punishing discrimination. Stupidity is not, or should not be, illegal.

Everyone has the right to do *anything* they want as long as it does not violate the identical rights of anyone else or violate a *voluntary* contractual agreement. Violate the rights of another person, and you are guilty. Sexual lifestyle does not figure into the equation anywhere.

Space Flight

Government-regulated and controlled space flight has accomplished *one* thing: it has kept humans earthbound longer than we otherwise would have been.

It is time to remove the regulatory roadblocks and let humans leave our planetary cradle. In fact, it is absolutely *necessary* if humans are to avoid extinction.

Let people experiment with launch vehicles without assuming they are building missiles with which to attack government facilities.

Let people experiment with new fuels and sources of power without kidnapping them for building a "weapon of mass destruction".

If, as many governments like to claim, humans are overpopulating the planet, having some voluntarily leaving for new frontiers would seem to be a wonderful solution. Just *try* to stop people from homesteading on other worlds once they get there, in defiance of government treaties that try to short-circuit property rights.

It all depends on getting government out of the way.

Which brings up the *real* reasons governments can not afford to let people emigrate from Earth: control and taxation.

Governments realize they would have no authority or *ability* to enforce "laws" and steal "taxes" from people who are beyond their grasp.

This loss of power scares them, and they are determined to make certain it *never* happens. But they *will* fail. Even if government gets off-planet first.

For the first time in human history, there is no relatively easily accessible frontier available for people who feel pressured by too much control. This is not a situation that is sustainable. If government doesn't step aside, tragedy will result. People don't need a government handout to leave Earth, they simply need government to get out of the way. Yet, even without government cooperation, it will happen. Will it be violent or will it be peaceful?

Suicide

All rights are at their core property rights, and all property rights begin with your right to own and control your own body and life. Ownership must *always* include to right to destroy that which you own.

If you use suicide to avoid responsibilities or obligations you voluntarily assumed, then you are not doing the right thing. Otherwise, while unpleasant, it is within your rights to decide to destroy your own life, as long as you harm no innocent person with your actions.

Some may claim that the emotional burden your death will place on others is "harm", but no one has a right to not be offended or saddened. Don't destroy or damage the property of anyone else with your act. Consider the consequences, and don't leave others with financial burdens that rightfully belong to you.

Consider alternatives, too. If it is truly that unbearable to "go on", why not just commit *virtual* suicide and walk away from your unbearable life and start fresh, doing things you never *dared* do before? After all, the worst that can happen is that your new life could kill you, right? You can always go through with your original plans later if you still feel the same.

Terrorism

The *worst possible* reaction to terrorism is to give the terrorists what they supposedly want: some of Americans' freedoms. When even *one* "minor" right is violated in response to a terrorist threat, the terrorists have won. The government is doing the terrorists' bidding *for* them.

Do you really think US troops in other countries are making America safer? Might they instead be giving new generations of people in those occupied countries a reason to grow up resenting, or even *hating*, America?

How would you feel if troops from North Korea were occupying your hometown, even benevolently, and trying to "win hearts and minds"? I assume most of us would be shooting them and setting "Improvised Explosive Devices".

If there is a need for a "military" beyond the "Constitutional militia" (*all* of us who live in America), which is doubtful, the place for them to be is *inside* America, on military bases, ready to "defend us" here, not scattered around the globe ensuring job security for the next generation of "terrorism fighters".

So, what to do besides getting troops out of every other country on the globe? ***More* liberty!** Don't play into the terrorist's hands by violating the liberty of Americans, but do the opposite and *eliminate* the various violations of liberty that *already* exist. No wiretapping, no reading emails, no tracing financial interactions.

And the one thing that would make the greatest, immediate difference: Get rid of any and all "laws" restricting guns; their features, possession, and sale, so that any terrorist would face a fully-armed population anytime he might wish to cause destruction. Anything less is only helping the terrorists.

Tobacco/Smoking

No one claims smoking is really *good* for your health. However, it is wrong to make smokers (and other tobacco users) become "second-class citizens" with "laws".

It is wrong to force businesses and their customers to obey a "smoke-free" policy if that is not what the business owner really wants. This violates the owner's right to use their own property as they see fit. Let the business owner decide whether to permit smoking or not.

Many people would *choose* to hang out in a smoke-filled bar, and many people would choose to hang out in one that *doesn't* allow smoking. I really can not fathom the expectation that a ***bar*** would offer a smoke-free environment; this seems almost as odd as a "no drinking" bar or a "food-free" restaurant. But, if there is a market for smoke-free bars, let people open them and freely compete with those which *permit* smoking.

No one can force people to work where they would rather not. If they don't want to breathe the smoke, they can find a job in a smoke-free place. Or, they *could* in a free society where choices were not as limited. Once again, government pretends to be the solution to problems that wouldn't exist without its meddling.

If you don't like to breathe second-hand smoke, avoid places where smoking is permitted by the owner. I do not smoke, but I have chosen to be in smoky places because the sacrifice was worth it to me at that time, in order to be with friends and attend events I was interested in. It was completely my choice, and I would have been cheated if that choice had been taken from me by "law".

If a smoker's smoke is bothering you outdoors, move to a different location. If a change of location isn't practical, then ask politely if they would mind not smoking for a while. Most people are willing to cooperate, unless you approach them with hostility or a sense of entitlement and superiority.

Of course, the government *loves* the money it extorts from tobacco users. Many non-smokers see nothing wrong with taking vast amounts of money from people who are doing something "they should be ashamed of". I don't agree. It is *wrong* to "tax" tobacco, especially to the point where the majority of the price that is paid goes to government. One solution: "bootlegging".

Although I am not a smoker, I sometimes grow tobacco simply because the government wants to control it. This is my way of providing tax-free tobacco, and defying The State in a small way. It feels good.

Trade Deficits

There is *no such thing* as a "trade deficit".   The truth is there can be *trade*, or there can be *theft*. The component that makes the distinction, by its presence or absence, is coercion.

The example that is much overused in regard to "trade deficits" is China. Chinese manufacturers make stuff, *cheap*, and sell it to customers in America. We customers pay them for it. No one forces us to buy any one thing in particular. Even government has so far failed in this area.

When we give a Chinese manufacturer dollars, we have made an even trade. Dollars for products. There is *no* deficit. Unless a government or mugger gets involved and takes your property (products or dollars) and gives nothing (or too little) in return, the trade is always an even one.

That is, unless you claim that the money you traded for the products is worth more than the product you got in return, in which case you are an idiot to agree to the trade. Personally, as an *individual*.

Or unless you wish to admit that US dollars are worthless (or worth-less), in which case the Chinese company got ripped off, not you.

You have no authority, nor enough wisdom, to judge another person's trade. What makes sense to them may seem one-sided to you. That is not for you to judge.

If you are mad that "PlastiCrap World" sells cheap Chinese products, *don't buy them*. Pay more and get a better item instead, either from the same store or from a competitor.

Or get what you want from a yard sale or flea market.

Or design and make your own.

I do all the above, and so can you. Plus, sometimes I just buy the "cheap junk" because it suits my needs at the price I am willing to pay at the time. Once again: voluntary trade; no deficit.

The whole myth of "trade deficits" is just an excuse to tell you who you can trade with, and under what conditions. It also *always* funnels some money into thieving governmental hands. This myth is an authoritarian power-grab and is bad for liberty and good for coercive government.

Transportation

The topic of transportation covers a lot of different areas. From roads, to railways, to airlines, to space travel, to vehicle design and production, to government-required permits and identification cards, to mass transit, and more.

Each has its own liberty-respecting solutions.

As an example: If "mass transit" is a needed service, let the free market meet the need. No *real* need (or *want*) will go unmet when someone could provide it for a profit.

It all comes down to the right to travel. The State has no authority to violate the right to travel, and has no authority to make people pay it a "cut" in order to exercise this right.

If government had *any* authority in this area, which it *doesn't*, it would only be in protecting the right of people to travel, and protecting them from aggressors and thieves along the road. Instead, government has become the primary *violator* of this right, and the employer of most of the dangerous highwaymen out on the roads today.

Trespassing

Any time a person is on property owned by another, and is there without permission of the owner, he is trespassing. It doesn't matter if it is a mistake, or intentional. Nor does it matter if the trespasser is lacking government papers showing "citizenship", or is a census worker or a DEA agent. It doesn't matter if the uninvited invader comes crawling under the fence on the back forty, or drives right up to the house and knocks on the front door.

If the intruder damages or steals any property while trespassing, then that is added to the offense, but the original violation- the *trespassing*- does not depend on any other harm being done.

Only privately owned property can be trespassed upon. Government property can not, since government owns nothing it did not steal from the true owners, or "purchase" with money it confiscated by coercion or that it counterfeited. Thieves do not *own* the property they possess, and their claims are without foundation.

In a free society you would deal with trespassers however you see fit. No one would have the authority to stop you, nor punish you for harming a person who was trespassing. And no one could punish you for whom you allow on your property.

Unemployment/Under-employment

In a free society, unemployment would be almost impossible. There would be no red tape, permits, fees, licenses, or competition-strangling "laws" preventing a person from engaging in trade.

If you had no job, or if you were unhappy with your employer, it would be a simple matter of setting up your own business in your spare room or garage.

Anything you wished to do to earn money would be OK as long as you didn't defraud anyone, and used no coercion against customers or competitors. Voluntary trade or services, between responsible people (responsible as determined by the parties concerned and not "society" at large), would be no one else's business.

What is it you have always wanted to do, but government somehow prevented you from doing? Are you *certain* it is government holding you back? Maybe it's time to get rid of the obstacles.

"Vice" (prostitution, gambling, "bad habits")

Not every "wrong" act should be a "crime". If, indeed, there were universal agreement that the act *is* wrong, which there never is on the minor stuff.

As long as responsible people reach a consensual agreement *without coercion* it is no one's business what they do. Not even if their behavior deeply offends someone.

This means, in part, that if it would not hurt any third party if done "for free", then it doesn't hurt any third party if done for pay.

It also means that even if the thing you want to do is harming *you*, no one else has a right to try to force you to stop, nor to charge you extra taxes "for your own good" to punish you for your behavior so that you might change.

If your act is harming your family, then they have a right to ask you to stop, or to break away from you, and even shun you if you refuse. If you use your "addiction" or bad choices as an excuse for stealing or for harming others, then they have a right to use defensive actions to stop you from harming them, physically or financially.

Be aware of the consequences of your choices, no matter what you do.

Violence

Many people talk about the problem of "violence". Violence is not a problem; the *incorrect use* of violence is a problem. Many times violence is the correct response to violence.

The **Zero Aggression Principle** reminds us that we have no right to *initiate force*. "Initiate", as in "start it". Even very young children recognize the clear difference between initiating force-*attacking*- and *responding* to an attack with force. "He started it" is often the cry for justice from their lips.

Violence used in self defense is not the same as violence used to hurt an innocent person. Initiated force (offensive violence or aggression) is wrong; reactive force (defensive violence) is just and *good*. An ethical individual will recognize the difference even while governments refuse to. This is one reason (out of many) the D.A.R.E. program is so evil; in its blanket condemnation of all violence, it does not differentiate between *initiated* force and *self defensive* force. That is because the "authorities" believe that only *they* can properly use violence; against *us*.

This blind rejection of self defensive violence has left our society crippled with predators; "criminals" *and* government.

Individuals intent on coercing and stealing, including those doing so under the auspices of government, will never learn to behave themselves if there are no painful or fatal consequences for their offenses.

We must reintroduce the predators among us to *fear*.

Violence in the form of self defense must be encouraged and rewarded, and people whom governments demonize for using self defense must be supported by all lovers of liberty.

Voting

"Don't vote. It only encourages them."

"If voting could change anything it would be illegal."

You've probably heard these quotes before. I would say, though, if it makes you *feel good* to vote, go ahead, but don't think for a second that by voting you are accomplishing anything beneficial to your individual liberty.

I have also heard the claim that those who don't vote have no right to complain. This is silly. Those who *do* vote are agreeing to abide by the results. Those who *do not* vote are not making that agreement. If *anyone* were giving up their right to complain, it would be the *voters*. However, no one ever really gives up that right.

Perhaps on a local level, and especially when a new "tax" or "law" is up for a vote, you might make a difference by voting in self defense, but on a national level your vote will not be counted, and your participation will be seen as a endorsement of the *status quo*.

Nationally, no candidate will ever be allowed to win no matter how many votes he or she gets (nor even to run a "serious" campaign) if that candidate seriously threatens the *status quo*. The Federal Election Commission, with its campaign "laws", is set up to prevent that from happening. It is a disappointing truth, but it *is* the truth.

If you vote, and stop there, you have done nothing to advance liberty. Possibly even less than nothing.

Instead, focus on how to increase the liberty in your own life, and in your sphere of influence, and let others worry about who will control the rudder on the train of government.

The time you spend thinking about voting, listening to the various lies told by the opposing politicians, and then actually going to vote, could be better spent on other things that make a real difference in your day-to-day life.

Don't let "working within the system" derail your life, liberty, and pursuit of happiness. Your rights, your *liberty*, are not up for a majority vote.

War

War is never a good situation for anyone intimately involved in it, even when undertaken in defense, and should be the absolute last resort.

However, war is big business for government, which observes from a safe distance in most cases, and it is flirted with far too casually. War empowers government to the detriment of individuals on all sides of the conflict.

War is justifiable *only* if you and your surroundings are being invaded and attacked- this is self defense. It is *not* justifiable to invade other people's property or kill them because of things some third party did to you. Even if you really think it's better to "fight them over there so you don't have to fight them here". Doing this is initiating force- it is *aggression*- and you lose the ethical high-ground by attacking others. Would you want to be held accountable for aggression committed by a government that you couldn't completely control? Neither should any other individuals anywhere.

If a political leader advocates an attack or an "act of war" he should be held *personally* responsible, along with only those who *personally* carry out the attack. "Collateral damage" is always wrong, and any innocent deaths that result are *murder.*

Welfare

Any "help" from government at any level is welfare. Don't berate a person on food stamps while collecting your Social Security or farm subsidies; there is *no* difference.

Welfare redistributes property stolen from productive people to those who, for whatever reason, are not productive enough to support themselves.

Welfare harms those it is taken from *and* those it is given to.

Charity, where money and time is given *voluntarily,* is much better for all involved. It is easier to expose those who simply want to take advantage of the help, and it is also less intrusive and dehumanizing for the deserving recipients.

Before government took over the work of charity, charity was very successful at meeting real needs. Even under government, most individuals are pretty charitable, although government has destroyed a lot of the motivation by fooling people into believing that charity is no longer necessary.

Government handouts all come with strings attached. You are required to let The State's agents pry into every nook and cranny of your life in exchange for the handouts. You are unconsciously encouraged to become dependent upon the "entitlements", and penalized for trying to improve your own condition.

The "welfare" comes at the cost of your self-ownership and dignity, and is a difficult trap to escape. By *design*.

Charity may be embarrassing. That is merely motivation to try to get to the point where you no longer need it. Charity does not require "contributions" from those who would rather keep their own money. It does not take other people's property without their consent. Those who may try to "scam the system" and collect charitable handouts are more easily discovered and cut off than those who do the same with welfare. Charity is self-correcting and self-regulating. Charity is superior in every possible way to welfare.

Accepting government handouts is like milking a grizzly bear. It may keep you fed for a while, and you may come to see the bear as your friend, but sooner or later you *will* get mauled.

It is better to avoid the bear, and look for voluntary help from charitable individuals and groups, even though government has put many of them out of business.

Some General Solutions

Here follow some general ideas that can be used to solve a wide range of problems.

These strike at the *root* of the problems that plague societies everywhere.

In some cases these are just concepts that, once understood, expose the lie that causes some problems.

In other cases these are specific things that can be adapted and used when confronted by a problem.

Abolition

We should *all* be abolitionists. Our mission is to abolish coercion as a socially acceptable foundation for society. Beginning within *ourselves*.

Those who fought to end racially-based slavery in the 19th Century were heading in the right direction, but stopped before their task was complete. We now carry on by fighting to strip away the veneer of legitimacy that has been crudely placed over acts such as theft, kidnapping, and murder by calling them "taxation", "arrest", and "war".

A person owns his own life and all the products of that life. A *slave* has this self-ownership violated by someone. Allowing government to dictate what you are allowed to do with your own body, and to force you to work to support government with the products of your labor, is still slavery. It is just as wrong as any *other* form of slavery.

Abolitionists recognize this terrible injustice, work to defeat it, speak out against it, and refuse to be silenced.

Arbitration

Even in a free society, conflicts will arise. When this happens, instead of turning to "The Law" to settle the differences, free people could seek arbitration.

I would imagine that many arbitrators would be available. They could advertise their services or rely on satisfied customers to recommend them to family and friends.

Those arbitrators who gain a reputation for wisdom and fairness would probably be easy for both parties to agree upon, unless one party in the dispute knows they are in the wrong.

Those arbitrators who did a poor job would find it difficult to attract new customers, since (unlike government-owned courts) there would be no monopoly, and people would have a choice.

The opposing individuals would need to find arbitration that is agreeable to both of them. If one party simply refused to agree to *any* arbitrator, this would constitute non-cooperation and the other party could move on to other options as if the uncooperative person had lost the arbitration.

When a judgment is made, there would probably be no enforcement mechanism in a *free* society.

Instead, those who are found to be at fault, if they refuse to correct the situation, would be subject to shunning, shaming, and picketing.

The harmed individual would be free to publicize both the *original* offense *as well as* the refusal to abide by the arbitration.

Current social media, and *future* developments in technology, would make publicizing an irresponsible individual (including his business operations) very simple. It would also make it very hard to run away from past offenses in order to start anew. This could make it difficult for the guilty party to function in society, where no one is forced to accommodate him in any way against their will.

In a free society, reputation would become much more important again.

After a few hard lessons, and some well-publicized examples, it might become obvious that without government for the bad guys to fall back on, cooperation and honesty are an easier and better strategy.

Reputation

In a future, *free*, society your reputation could become your most valuable asset, or your biggest liability. Not necessarily your *sexual* reputation, but your reputation for following through and doing what you say you will do, and for not attacking people.

Online auction sites, like eBay, allow people to rate others they interact with. Over the course of time you begin to see who is a safe bet to do business with, and who is a risk. Those who are more of a risk may have to lower their price to attract those willing to take a chance in order to save some money. The best bet is to do what you say you will do, or avoid doing business where a good reputation is needed. Those places could get more scarce as time passes and technology advances.

If you have a reputation for initiating force it could become hard to find people who will hire you. They would have to consider their liability in sending a known aggressor out to represent them in society.

If you do something that could negatively affect your reputation, you would have a big incentive to make it right.

I imagine that competing businesses would spring up to compile and track a person's reputation score, which could be accessed much as a credit score is currently. Those who didn't prove as accurate as their competitors would need to improve their data, or go out of business.

A good reputation could be groomed like a good credit score is, and credit scores would probably comprise a part of the overall reputation. You might jump at a chance to do good things that would increase your score, while avoiding things that might harm it.

There would probably arise a system to cater to those whose reputations have not been so well-maintained. For a price. Opportunities abound when liberty is the driving force.

Restitution

Restitution should be the goal for those acts of aggression, theft, or fraud that self-defense failed to stop.

Restitution should be the primary goal of *any* justice system.

Obviously there are instances where restitution is *not* possible, such as when irreversible bodily harm has been done or where death occurs, but in most cases it *is*.

Restitution is the paying off of a debt that was incurred by some act that causes harm- coercion or theft. This does not violate the rights of the debtor since he *voluntarily* took on this debt by his actions. He may have thought he would never have to *pay* the debt, but it was still his choice to take it on.

However, in a society free from coercion, it may not be possible to collect from someone who simply doesn't care about his reputation or obligations. In this case shunning, even to the point of *death*, might be the solution. **It makes much more sense than prison.** In cases like these, I would like to see "victims' compensation charities" form to help out those whose violators fail to fulfill their obligations.

Rights

Do you really know what a "right" is? Often we hear people saying they have a "right" to this or that (such as governmentally-provided health care or other subsidies), and sometimes it almost sounds like they might have a point. However, it is easy to tell a right from a "gimme", if you know the nature of rights.

A right is something you can do, without asking permission from anyone, simply because you are alive. Anything that does not violate another person's identical and equal rights is within your rights to do, whether trivial or monumentally important (and *obviously*, regardless of whether or not it is mentioned in the Bill of Rights). A right can only be respected or violated. It can not be limited, regulated, restricted, licensed, or taxed- as all these are just different ways of violating the right.

A right does not place an obligation on anyone else on your behalf, and "having to put up with being offended" by your actions does not equal an "obligation" on anyone else. In other words, as long as you are not harming or threatening to harm any innocent person while you exercise your right it doesn't matter how upset, offended, or "scared" someone gets by your actions. They have no right to try to stop you.

No one has to *provide* you with the means to exercise your right, either. That part is up to you.

The Bill of Rights was seriously misnamed as it did nothing to "give" you rights, but was simply written and ratified to make it illegal for government, at *any* level (yes, even *without* the 14th Amendment- read the Constitution- Article IV, Section 2- if you don't believe me.) to make any "laws" in an attempt to violate anyone's *pre-existing* rights (a redundant phrase).

For example: You don't have "Second Amendment rights", the government has "Second Amendment *limits*". That they choose to illegally and illegitimately ignore and violate those limits by acting in prohibited ways doesn't affect your rights in the least. It only affects your *liberty*, which is the freedom to exercise those rights.

Private individuals are not prohibited from violating your rights by the Bill of Rights, but by the nature of rights and by the fact that your rights do not exist at their whim. Their rights do not nullify your rights in any way. Anyone- whether a government thug, a private individual, or an employer- who chooses to violate your rights in any way, using any justification, is not your friend, but a mortal enemy. If they do not trust you as a fully-functional human being with all your rights intact, they do not trust you at all and you should not trust them either.

Shunning

You have the right to associate with anyone you want. You also have the right to *refuse* to associate with anyone you do not want around you - for *any* reason.

You own yourself and you can (and probably *should*) choose who to let into your life. Your reasons may be good, or they may be stupid or wrong, but the right is still yours. Others also have the right to choose to not associate with *you*, so don't engage in arbitrary shunning lightly.

Remember that if you decide to shun a person because of his race or religion or because he likes cats, others may use *that* decision as a reason to shun *you*. Both people who share the trait you dislike, and those who simply disagree with your reasons for shunning him. I would refuse to associate with anyone whom I discovered was discriminating against (through shunning) anyone who was not guilty of initiating force, fraud, or theft. I suspect others would do the same.

Government agents and employees are a prime target for shunning. The State tries to violate your right to associate with whom you choose in every way possible, usually by forcing its minions upon you. That is a good justification for shunning them.

Zero Aggression Principle

"No human being has the right - under any circumstances - to initiate force against another human being, nor to threaten or delegate its initiation."

This version of The Zero Aggression Principle (ZAP), formulated by L. Neil Smith, is generally (but not universally) agreed to be the core principle of libertarian philosophy. Personally, I *DO* think this is the foundation of libertarianism. This is how you show your respect for the self-ownership of those around you. If you follow this principle, you may not be a *perfect* person, but you would probably be a pretty good neighbor. You would definitely be a good example of true libertarianism.

The ZAP has the same message as The Golden Rule and most other guides for dealing ethically with others; each culture has its own way of saying basically the same thing.

I have heard the argument that "initiating force" can be defined any way the person wishes to define it. I do not believe this. Even small children understand the concept of "he started it"

Someone calling you a nasty name has *not* initiated force; someone pointing a gun at you *has*. Only someone physically attacking you or making a credible threat to do so has initiated force. I don't see that it is a difficult concept to grasp. Once force has been initiated you have the right to counter that force with defensive actions, *including* force.

You *may* have an ethical obligation to use an appropriate amount of force. In other words, if someone shoves you, you can't justify beating that person to death. In most common situations like this, you would probably be smart to simply walk away. However, this is not always an option an aggressor will leave you. You might need to point a gun at that person and warn them to leave or be shot. At that point, they have a choice to leave or to escalate the situation.

Some people may claim that this is "Utopian" but I *know* it works, for *real*, in everyday life. I have never run across a situation where it failed to provide the proper perspective in dealing with others.

If you don't want to accept it, you can sit around and formulate all sorts of "what if" scenarios that you will probably never face. That just shows me that you have a desire to keep open the option of attacking someone you don't like, even if they have *not* attacked you first. That is a sign that you may not be a trustworthy, or nice, person.

Now, this leads to another prickly issue that some people don't quite understand: just because you have *no **right*** to initiate force doesn't mean that in some cases you couldn't decide to do so *anyway* and then take whatever consequences come your way.

Only you, with an understanding that you are stepping *outside of what you have a **right** to do*, can evaluate the situation which confronts you. If you believe your actions are necessary and the consequences of *not* acting would be worse than the consequences of acting beyond your rights, you should do what you believe you *must* and accept the consequences.

Appendix

Definitions:

Anarchy- When I use the word "anarchy", I am using the original usage: **without** (*an-*) **king/ruler** (*archos*). This doesn't mean, to me, a free-for-all. This means *YOU* are responsible for all your actions and accept *ALL* the consequences of those actions. It means you have accepted your basic human responsibility to govern yourself, instead of abdicating to some external coercive force (a Ruler or a government).

I realize that the dictionary has a lot of "chaos" mixed in with its definitions of "anarchy", but that is not *ever* what I mean when *I* use the word. If you have a better word, just substitute that when I write "anarchy".

Arrest- "Arrest" is the euphemism for a kidnapping committed by government employees while they are "on the clock".

Coercion- All *initiated* force is coercion, but not all coercion necessarily involves force.

A lot of coercion uses deceit or manipulation. Not all force is *coercion*. Some force is justifiable, such as in self defense (it is not "initiated force" in this case), but what I call "coercion" is never justified.

I don't include self-defensive actions as coercion (by definition), even if you are able to "talk" a thug out of attacking you by *lying* to him. He initiated the force- he is the aggressor- so your actions are strictly self-defense.

For me, coercion is purely the initiatory act of forcing or causing someone to act in a way that is against their legitimate will.

"Common good"- "Common" in this case means "collective", rather than "ordinary". Its meaning is closer to "communist" or "everyone" than to the more "common" meaning. "General welfare" is another way to say the same thing.

What is "good"? Good is something that actively helps or benefits someone who is not being harmful to others. It isn't just an absence of "evil" since there are neutral acts that are neither "good" nor "evil", such as walking across the room. It is never "good" to help harm innocent people. This is an excellent reason to refuse to help the police. Ever.

So, "the common good" (or "general welfare") would be something that helps "everyone".

The only way to help "everyone" is to help each individual. Yet, most of the time "the common good" is invoked as an excuse to *harm* the individual. When that individual is not deserving harm right now, the act of harming him is evil.

Violating the rights of an individual; taking away the liberty of an individual, except as an act of individual self-defense, is not serving "the common good" in any way. It only serves The State and other parasites. Instead of imagining you are helping the majority, you need to think about the minority you are harming. That is the true measure of the "good" of your acts. It is better to do *nothing* (and therefore fail to help some people) than to do *something* which harms some who do not deserve to be harmed right now. Respecting rights is the only true common good.

Freedom- "Freedom" means doing what you want to do.

Freedom is morally neutral; it can be good or it can be bad- depending upon your desires. You have an obligation to not use your freedom to act upon any desires to harm the innocent, and also to accept the responsibility for your actions. You are accountable for *everything* you do.

Other people, consequences, responsibilities, "laws", beliefs, reality, and many other things can limit your freedom. Freedom, liberty, and rights are not the same thing but are entangled.

Some people can be perfectly "free" in prison, while others couldn't be free in Utopia.

Government- "Government" is an organization of individuals who attempt to make the rules for a particular geographical area. Regardless of their claims, they are *not* voluntary or consensual, as "voting" and other participatory acts can never really make a substantive difference because of the rules which the government has established to regulate the election process.

Governments allow no competition with the organization and no opting out. Government is financed through "taxation", which is merely statist-speak for "theft by government". It holds a monopoly on the use of force, enforced by its own enforcers and backed up by the courts it runs. Because government enforces the rules that limit its power, there is really no limit to what it can get away with, given time.

Innocent- A person is "innocent" if they do not deserve to be harmed right now; at this moment.

The only reason anyone would deserve to be

harmed at any time is if they are in the process of attacking, robbing, or defrauding an innocent person, or possibly trespassing.

Everyone is innocent sometimes, and *no one* is innocent all the time. If you are initiating force or using coercion you are not innocent.

Libertarian- A libertarian is someone who abides by the *Zero Aggression Principle.*

A libertarian values individual rights and liberty and respects them in others even if they are inconvenient; seeking to always maximize liberty.

I would also include the qualifications that they do not practice defrauding others (keeps his word), and not otherwise seek solutions in coercion. *Ever.*

Not even by using hired thugs wearing the silly hat of government.

Self defensive actions are not "aggression" or "initiation" of anything other than self defense, but are a result of the aggression or deception of others.

A libertarian does not wish to control others, not even "nicely" or for their own good. Instead he should mind his own business as long as no one is being attacked or harmed.

Voluntary interactions between responsible people are no one else's business no matter how much their actions may offend you. Libertarians respect this.

I recognize libertarian to be the same as *anarchist* to be the same as *sovereign individual* to be the same as *"live and let live"*, and to be "the only true standard of consistently ethical behavior"; the only *right* way to live.

If you hyphenate "libertarian" with something else that compromises the foundational principles in *any* way, however "minor", then you have negated the "libertarian" part of your name in its entirety. It is really much simpler than many people would have you believe. When a person fails to live up to this description in some areas, in those areas he falls short of being "libertarian".

Liberty- "Liberty" is simply the freedom to exercise your rights.

Rights- A "right" is something you can do just because you exist. It is not dependent upon anyone's permission. Anything that you can do without violating the *equal* rights of another individual is your right to do, no matter how trivial or how important. A real right can not impose an obligation on someone else.

Rights do not come from anyone else, nor from government, nor from any document.

A right can either be respected or it can be violated, but it can not be limited, regulated, licensed, rationed, or otherwise turned into a privilege. A privilege is the *opposite* of a right.

Having a right doesn't mean there will be no consequences for *exercising* that right. There are always consequences and responsibilities for every action. Just because you have a right to do something does not mean it is the best thing to do right now. Think before you act, or even better, before you *need* to act.

The End.

Other books by **Kent S McManigal**

Indy-Pindy, The Liberty Mouse
(tinyurl.com/IndyPindy)
> An introduction to liberty, responsibility, and independence for young readers.

Kent's Liberty Primer
(tinyurl.com/KentsLiberty)
> A handbook for understanding liberty and rights, and why they matter

Tao Liberty Ching
(tinyurl.com/TaoLiberty)
> Short refrains illuminating the path to liberty

Sandy's Legacy
(tinyurl.com/SandyQuail)
> A "pets and nature" book about the quail who shared Kent McManigal's teenage years, illustrated by the author

Contact me at **dullhawk@hotmail.com**
> As long as I am alive, online, and email formats don't change, I will keep this email address

CPSIA information can be obtained
at www.ICGtesting.com
Printed in the USA
LVHW080500090919
630382LV00018B/201/P

9 781453 742822